THE
SHAKESPEAREAN
ETHIC

THE
SHAKESPEAREAN
ETHIC

John Vyvyan

SHEPHEARD-WALWYN (PUBLISHERS) LTD

First published in 1959 by
Chatto & Windus, London

This edition published 2011 by
Shepheard-Walwyn (Publishers) Ltd
107 Parkway House, Sheen Lane,
London SW14 8LS
www.shepheard-walwyn.co.uk

British Library Cataloguing in Publication Data
A catalogue record of this book
is available from the British Library

ISBN: 978-0-85683-284-0

Cover design by ML Design, London (www.ml-design.co.uk)
Based on a stained glass window reproduced courtesy of
The School of Economic Science, London
Photography © Richard Wythe

Typeset by Alacrity, Chesterfield, Sandford, Somerset
Printed and bound in the United Kingdom
by Short Run Press Ltd, Exeter

The tradition of modern thought presents philosophy as asking at the outset of its task three vital questions: What can we know? What ought we to do? What may we hope? The second of these is recognised as the fundamental problem of ethics.

Ethics, NICOLAI HARTMANN

Mind, from the supreme heights a kindred mind calls to thee, that thou be a dividing mean betwixt the low deities and Jove.

Lose not thy rights; nor, downward hurled and falling to the depths, plunge to the waters of black Acheron.

To His Own Spirit, GIORDANO BRUNO

TO
MY MOTHER

Contents

Publishers' Note

THIS IS AN ENTIRELY NEW edition of John Vyvyan's insightful book in that the entire text has been reset, but without alteration except for the addition of chapter titles to indicate the content.

However, some additions have been made which we hope will enhance the usefulness of this edition. Having been educated in Switzerland, John Vyvyan was clearly familiar with the great literature of Italy, France and Germany and has sometimes made a point by quoting from Goethe or Dante, for example, in the original. For the benefit of readers less familiar with these languages, we have added translations as footnotes. We appreciate that translations can never be as apt as the original but we hope they will be useful.

Vyvyan illustrates his argument with many quotations from Shakespeare's plays. To assist in finding where they appear in the respective plays, we have listed the first line of the quotations at the end of the book and relied on the Oxford University Press edition of The Complete Works for the references. There is also a short list of the books to which Vyvyan refers. Finally, the index has been considerably enlarged.

I

Principles of Construction
in the Tragedies

IT IS STRIKING that Shakespeare's tragic characters are continually asking themselves questions. In their soliloquies, they weigh up alternative courses of action, and the question is implicit, What ought I to do?

In the opinion of some critics, however, for us to ask such a question is illegitimate. The critical argument is, that since what Hamlet or Brutus actually did was dramatically excellent, it was therefore, within our terms of reference, right. That is true, from its own standpoint; but it has this flaw: by limiting the problem to aesthetics and the theatre, it leaves out Shakespeare. From the evidence of the sonnets alone, which were probably not intended for publication, we see that Shakespeare was himself a 'perturbed spirit'. He was not satisfied with conventional answers; yet he needed answers, for his own peace, in terms of life. And his plays are part of his quest for them.

Why do we enjoy tragedy? Partly, as Aristotle suggests, because it helps us to 'gather the meaning of things'. A modern audience seeing, let us say, *Macbeth*, is unlikely to be much stirred by pity or terror. But we may feel that something from the deeps has been revealed; and it is not only Macbeth's soul that we then know better, but our own; because the figures of the drama are not unlike transformation symbols between the conscious mind and the unconscious. But if seeing a tragedy has helped us to understand ourselves better, that is because it has brought over to consciousness things that our unconscious already knew. It is like Plato's doctrine of reminiscence: what seems like new knowledge has, in fact, been brought out of ourselves.

If an audience has this experience, it is far more intense for an author; and it is the curious fascination of bringing forth wisdom from himself that chiefly impels him to write. A poet does not write to set down things he clearly knows, but to open the lips of his own oracle. Rhythm helps him to establish communication with the unconscious; and it is more for purposes of discovery than presentation that poetry is rhythmical.

In their uninspired moments, poets may long for fame and wealth; but these incentives have nothing to do with the production of poetry; not even their opposites, derision and poverty, can keep a poet from his task when the forms of the unconscious are demanding expression. *Fiat tragoedia, ruat caelum.** There is also, of course, a resistance to expression; so that to write tragedy is like wrestling with a dark angel and compelling him to reveal himself. In the throes of this struggle, mundane motives cease to count. It is true that Shakespeare was capable of mercenary as well as sublime thoughts; but from the critical point of view this is an unproductive vein. It is irrelevant to criticism that Shakespeare was successful; if his work had led him to misery, like poor Greene, he would have done it, or died.

* 'Let the tragedy be played out, though the heavens should fall.'

We must, however, distinguish between inspiration and intention. They stand in contrast, as the unconscious to the conscious mind. It is possible to have too much of either; too much adherence to intention tends to artificiality, and too much inspiration to mediumship. It is not the least of Shakespeare's qualities that he is able to balance these opposites so finely. But what we must consider first is intention.

What ought Hamlet or Brutus to do – something that will make a good play, or something that will lead to a good life? I am sure that both these questions are important. It is obvious that Shakespeare aimed at dramatic excellence; but it is equally clear – unless we prefer to be blind to it – that he was deeply concerned with the meaning and enhancement of life. What the tragic hero did may have been theatrically right; but if it was ethically wrong, that also was Shakespeare's preoccupation. And a study of this second point may lead us to a better understanding of himself. Our need for this is brought home by Bradley's astonishing remark: 'We cannot be sure, as with those other poets we can, that in his works he expressed his deepest and most cherished convictions on ultimate questions, or even that he had any. And in his dramatic conceptions there is enough to occupy us.'* This statement is a challenge in itself. And I hope to show that Shakespeare had convictions, that he expressed them, and that they are so related to his dramatic conceptions as to be mutually revealing. In fact, the ethical problem seems to have exercised an increasing fascination over him; and in his later plays, when he knew all the tricks of the theatre

* Bradley, 'Shakespearian Tragedy', Lecture I.

and could probably have gone from strength to strength in the production of theatrical success, he wittingly sacrificed stage effect in order to pursue the ethical as distinct from the dramatic problem. These later plays are more seldom staged, but Shakespeare was not in his dotage; it is simply that in them he was less concerned with the art of the theatre than with the science of life. The ethical interest had always been with him, and it is from this standpoint that we shall proceed.

Shakespeare allows his characters, nearly always, to express their own philosophy, and we cannot identify him personally with any one of them. Occasionally, however, he slips in a few lines which we may feel come straight from him to us; but we can only be sure of this if they express ideas that are consistently developed in successive plays. To trace a few of these continuing themes is one of the aims of this book.

It may sound platitudinous to say that only a careful study of the context can tell us what Shakespeare intends a word to mean; but a surprising amount of confusion has been caused by failing to distinguish between Shakespeare's values and those of his characters. Words like honour, nobility, justice, traitor and harlot are often, perhaps more often than not, to be suspected in this connection. Sometimes, but comparatively seldom, this is obvious. Ophelia, Desdemona and Hermione are all called harlots by the hero, and it is clear that he is self-deceived. But when we notice how frequently justice, as the speaker terms it, is to Shakespeare tyranny or worse, how often honour, in its conventional sense, is deliberately shown by Shakespeare as preventing conciliation and conducing to superfluous death, we come to mistrust the face value of many other words and to consider them in a wider context of ideas. Gradually this leads us to a persisting standard of value, for Shakespeare was no chameleon in his principles; and it is not unreasonable to hope that, although we may never know much about his life, it will be possible some day to establish his philosophy. But we must begin by being sure, as Bradley was not, that he had one.

Any characteristics that recur in play after play are important to this enquiry. I should like to consider, first of all, Shakespeare's method of presenting tragedy. In all presentation there is an element of showmanship, but a great deal more is here involved. Any attempt to fit Shakespeare's tragedies to the Aristotelean pattern is to lay them on a Procrustean bed, for Shakespeare worked out a pattern of his own. Much of this has been thoroughly mapped* and it would be supererogatory to go over well-trodden ground. But there are some other principles of construction in the tragedies which, so far as I know, have not been isolated and to which Shakespeare is remarkably faithful. I will summarise what I conceive these to be, and attempt to justify the statement later.

FIRST: We are shown a soul, in many respects noble, but with a fatal flaw, which lays it open to a special temptation.

SECOND: The 'voices' of the coming temptation are characterised for us, so that we may have no doubt that they will persuade to evil.

THIRD: There is a temptation scene, in which the weak

---

* See T. W. Baldwin: *William Shakespeare's Five-Act Structure*, University of Illinois Press, 1947.

spot of the hero's soul is probed, and the temptation is yielded to.

FOURTH: We are shown an inner conflict, usually in the form of a soliloquy, in which the native nobility of the hero's soul opposes the temptation, but fails.

FIFTH and SIXTH: There is a second temptation and a second inner conflict, of mounting intensity, with the result that the hero loses the kingship of his own soul.

SEVENTH: The tragic act, or act of darkness.

EIGHTH: The realisation of horror.

NINTH: Death.

This is Shakespeare's own way of conceiving tragedy, and it has little to do with Aristotle. I will illustrate this briefly from *Macbeth*. I do not mean to discuss the play, but merely to show that it contains the pattern.

Macbeth, before he enters, has cast his shadow on the scene. The full measure of it can only be taken after we have established Shakespeare's standard from several plays, and I must ask the reader's patience if some statements seem arbitrary here. Support for them has yet to be built; and this cannot be done from a single tragedy. The opening scene is as short as it well could be, and yet there is much more in it than atmosphere. There is an under-meaning in the words of the witches that they will meet Macbeth on the heath when the battle – his great victory – has been 'lost and won'. The battle is then in progress, and the witches know that Macbeth, although winning in one sense, has already begun to lose in another; that is the reason why the hour has come to tempt him. Shakespeare doubtless had in mind a text he has illustrated several times – that it is possible to gain the world and to lose one's soul. We are about to witness the tragedy of a man who will lose to win; and in order to do so, he must invert his values, 'Fair is foul and foul is fair.' This is one of the constants of Shakespearean tragedy. The inversion of values is shown taking place in every tragic hero, but he is generally unconscious of it.

The witches, who are themselves psychic phenomena, alert us to the fact that two battles are really taking place; and the more important, philosophically, is that within Macbeth. His state of soul is shown to us, symbolically, before he comes on stage. 'What bloody man is that?' Then we are told of his recent exploits; of 'his brandish'd steel which smoked with bloody execution'; of how, when he met the rebel, 'he unseam'd him from the nave to the chaps', and fixed his head on the battlements. And the savagery is summed up, as if it were 'to bathe in reeking wounds, or memorise another Golgotha'. To the hearers, all this is heroic; but, as may be shown from other plays, it is a form of madness to Shakespeare:

> I have made you mad;
> And even with such-like valour men hang and drown
> Their proper selves.

'Proper selves' represents another Shakespearean constant of which we shall have more to say. Temptation is resisted when the 'proper self' is in command; but when it is not, which is a kind of madness, the temptation is yielded to. Macbeth, by giving rein to a blood-lust that is linked with Golgotha, has become a man who 'is not with himself' and therefore he is predisposed to fall.

The voices of temptation – the witches first, and Lady Macbeth later – are obviously persuading to evil.

The first temptation is by the witches. We must remember that *Macbeth*, written in 1606, comes late in Shakespeare's tragedies, and he was able to handle such scenes with great economy. What the witches say is brief and equivocal; but it is temptation beyond doubt. Banquo says, 'Good sir, why do you start, and seem to fear?' Macbeth starts because the witches have touched the flaw in his soul. They did not sow the evil seed, but watered it. It is the guilt of an idea already present that he fears. And then we are told his fault – 'the royal hope, that he seems rapt withal'.

With great concision, the fruit of long experience in temptation scenes, Shakespeare has presented the essential points: the background weakness of the hero's soul, the nature of the temptation, and the implication that, if he follows his fate, he will yield. But it must be stressed – although to do so here is to anticipate – that no Shakespearean hero is compelled to follow his fate; there is always a spiritual quality in him which, if it is asserted as it ought to be, is superior to fate. 'My fate cries out!' may be Shakespeare's indication that a temptation is in progress; but to follow a ghost is the opposite of asserting the soul's supremacy. This is looking too far ahead; enough, for the moment, that Macbeth is being tempted to follow the witches: 'Would they had stayed!'

The first inner conflict is then revealed to us in Macbeth's asides:

This supernatural soliciting
Cannot be ill, cannot be good ...
If good, why do I yield to that suggestion
Whose horrid image doth unfix my hair
And make my seated heart knock at my ribs,

8

Against the use of nature? Present fears
Are less than horrible imaginings:
My thought, whose murder yet is but fantastical,
Shakes so my single state of man that function
Is smother'd in surmise, and nothing is
But what is not.

Instead of sovereignty of the proper self, there is an insur-
rection in his soul; and the tragic inversion is continuing,
so that 'nothing is but what is not'.

The second temptation is by Lady Macbeth. Its place in
the pattern is all we need to notice about it at the
moment.

The second inner conflict is integrated with the temptation – a point of construction we will consider later –
and is revealed in soliloquy:

If it were done when 'tis done, then 'twere well
It were done quickly; if the assassination
Could trammel up the consequence, and catch
With his surcease success; that but this blow
Might be the be-all and the end-all here,
But here, upon this bank and shoal of time,
We'd jump the life to come. But in these cases
We still have judgment here; that we but teach
Bloody instructions, which, being taught, return
To plague the inventor ...

The temptation is then intensified, and the final battle
'lost and won' – a spiritual defeat, accompanied by an outward show of resolution:

I am settled, and bend up
Each corporal agent to this terrible feat.

We are still on the bloodstained path to Golgotha.

The three other phases of the sequence – the tragic act, the realisation of horror and the hero's death – all clearly follow in due order.

We may pause to notice, here, that the tragic act comes early in *Macbeth*, midway in *Julius Caesar*, near the end in *Othello*, and right at the end in *Hamlet*. It is most unlikely that this is accidental. Shakespeare's choice of plots is not haphazard. I suggest that he selected and shaped these in order to give himself the opportunity to analyse, in detail, each stage of his tragic path. *Macbeth* is a deep study of the aftermath of the deed of darkness, of the realisation of horror and the relentless approach of the reckoning of death. *Othello* particularly examines the temptation; that is why Iago is a much more developed character than the witches or Hamlet's ghost. *Hamlet* is almost wholely concerned with the inner conflict.

2

Macbeth, Julius Caesar: The Temptation

N O ONE DOUBTS that Macbeth and Othello ought not to have done what they did. The general comment on *Othello* is, 'O, the pity of it!' And on *Macbeth*, 'Oh, horror! horror! horror!' But about the assassination of Caesar there has always been a division of opinion. Brutus can, and does, support his action upon ethical grounds. Are they valid; or rather, since that is our enquiry, did Shakespeare think they were?

It has been said that Shakespeare does not take sides in *Julius Caesar*. But this is not so. Each of his major plays is (besides being so many other things) a study in morals. Shakespeare is never ethically neutral. He is never in doubt as to whether the souls of his characters are rising or falling. *Julius Caesar* is really the tragedy of Brutus; and Caesar's last reproachful question has an under-meaning; in this sense it is not a question, but a statement and a prophecy, *'Et tu, Brute!'* Before the play opens, 'Brutus was Caesar's angel'. At its close, Caesar's ghost is to him, 'Thy evil spirit, Brutus.' How great a fall from grace! But if we set the play beside the tragic sequence – which, I believe, Shakespeare looked upon as his rules of tragedy – we are not surprised that Brutus fell. He falls by the pattern. Let us trace this out.

The fatal flaw in the soul of Brutus, as Shakespeare displays it to us, is that he puts politics before humanity: that he has more faith in the power of death than in the power of love. More than once we are told that there is mutual love between himself and Caesar; but Brutus never assays its influence. '... I love him well.' 'It must be by his death ...' That juxtaposition begins to reveal Brutus. It does not even occur to him that a political situation might be met in terms of humanity and life. His weak point, which the temptation probes, is that he sets what we now call an ideology higher than love and life.

The voice of the temptation is clearly characterised, so that we may know for certain that to follow its council will be to fall. Shakespeare is showing us his own thoughts when he describes the tempter. 'Yond' Cassius has a lean and hungry look ...', and '... he hears no music'. The man who has no music in his soul, 'Is fit for treasons, strategems and spoils ...', and, therefore, he is very dangerous. Cassius confirms both points – the weakness in Brutus and the evil in himself – in a soliloquy that would be surprisingly candid, if it were not intended as a signpost to the audience:

Well, Brutus, thou art noble; yet, I see,
Thy honourable metal may be wrought
From that it is disposed: therefore, it is meet
That noble minds keep ever with their likes,
For who so firm that cannot be seduced?

He has tied the label of seducer on himself. If Brutus continues in such company, he will gradually be corrupted.

Shakespeare is following his pattern; and shows, by doing so, that he is not neutral.

The first temptation stands out clearly against this background. And the first inner conflict, of which there are several intimations, comes to a head in the soliloquy, 'It must be by his death.'

The second temptation is by means of the anonymous letters which are thrown into his house from the street. And to this, again, Brutus yields:

> O Rome, I make thee promise ...

He has scarcely uttered the words, when he is plunged into the second inner conflict. The soliloquy in which this is mirrored is most important, because it also sheds light on other plays:

> Since Cassius first did whet me against Caesar,
> I have not slept.
> Between the acting of a dreadful thing
> And the first motion, all the interim is
> Like a phantasma or a hideous dream:
> The Genius and the mortal instruments
> Are then in council, and the state of man,
> Like to a little kingdom, suffers then
> The nature of an insurrection.

This could be said of all Shakespeare's tragic heroes, and it states his own theory of the conditions which must lead up to every tragic act. We have already found them in Macbeth:

> My thought, whose murder yet is but fantastical,
> Shakes so my single state of man that function
> Is smother'd in surmise, and nothing is
> But what is not.

When the evil voices have been listened to, and are allowed to re-echo in the mind, they create the thoughts that are traitors. These, like the soldiers in the Trojan horse, capture the citadel from within. What the tragic hero is now losing is, in Swinburne's perfect phrase, 'the Lordship of the soul'. Shakespeare pictures the soul as a kingdom (potentially the kingdom of heaven) wherein man's true self should be enthroned. The outcome of the inner warfare, which always follows the yielding to temptation, is that the ruler within is overthrown. The Genius now controls the mortal instruments; and the Genius, in this sense, is a usurping power, the inspiration of the deed of darkness. The tragic act is never consummated in the physical world until the lordship of the inner world has been lost.

It is because Shakespeare makes these assumptions that we find, if we analyse his tragedies, that he has his laws and follows them; but they are not Aristotelean. First, there is the battle within, and the losing of it precipitates the tragedy:

> Yield up, O Love, thy crown and hearted throne
> To tyrannous hate!

The relationship between love and the self, as Shakespeare defines it, we must examine later. Meanwhile, it is clear that Brutus, Othello and Macbeth all describe a similar experience as they undergo it.

The defeat of the spirit is often shown as an extinguishing of light. This, too, is important in several plays, and merits a short digression. Shakespeare uses light in a way we might call sacramental, as the outward sign of the inward grace. And the hero turns away from light before the tragic crime. Macbeth:

> Stars, hide your fires;
> Let not light see my black and deep desires.

And again, before the murder of Banquo, he says:

> Come, seeling night,
> Scarf up the tender eye of pitiful day,
> And with thy bloody and invisible hand
> Cancel and tear to pieces that great bond
> Which keeps me pale! Light thickens, and the crow
> Makes wing to the rooky wood ...

Othello, also, is an enemy of light:

> Put out the light, and then put out the light:
> If I quench thee, thou flaming minister,
> I can again thy former light restore,
> Should I repent me; but once put out thy light,
> Thou cunning'st pattern of excelling nature,
> I know not where is that Promethean heat
> That can thy light relume.

But the tragic hero may also show a hunger for light, which springs from the intuition that it would save him – if he could obtain it. But he fails. Whenever Shakespeare's characters call for, 'Lights!' – as after the play scene in *Hamlet*, when the whole stage takes up the cry, 'Lights! Lights!' – it is as if Shakespeare were telling us of a despairing need for inward illumination. And when they cannot see the physical light, or when it is unnatural as in *Richard III*:

The lights burn blue.
Cold fearful drops stand on my trembling flesh.

Or when they extinguish it deliberately:

Out, out, brief candle!

Then we may know, as if Shakespeare had whispered in our ear, that they are stumbling in spiritual darkness towards the precipice where they will surely fall.

The sacrament of light is used most tellingly in the case of Brutus. There is a nobility in him that will not easily consent to darkness. It is the day of the assassination, but it is not yet daylight. A storm is raging, with flashes of lightning. Brutus is up; but he cannot see, he tells us, 'the progress of the stars'. He is in darkness without and within. Then he calls to the sleeping boy, whose name is light:

Lucius, ho! Lucius, I say! When, Lucius, when? Awake! Get me a taper in my study, Lucius. When it is lighted, come and call me.

What an invocation! But it is not by the light of the taper, which Lucius brings, that he reads the anonymous letter, thrown in to tempt him further. As with Richard, 'the lights burn blue', when he says:

The exhalations whizzing in the air
Give so much light that I may read by them.

That is the prelude to the second temptation. The conspirators arrive, 'their faces buried in their cloaks', adding a deeper darkness to the night; and then Shakespeare, with the same symbolism, gives us his own judgment on the plot itself. The dawn of Caesar's death-day is about to break. Decius speaks:

Here lies the east: doth not the day break here?
Casca: No.
Cinna: O, pardon, sir, it doth –
Casca: You shall confess that you are both deceived.
Here, as I point my sword, the sun arises.

That is the faction: about to put Rome, and the whole world to rights, they do not know the direction of the sunrise. And they look for it, not in heaven, but on the point of a sword. For Brutus, the lights have gone out; and he knows it, in his soul:

O, conspiracy ...
Where wilt thou find a cavern dark enough
To mask thy monstrous visage? Seek none, conspiracy;
Hide it in smiles and affability.

He might have been quoted by Macbeth:

False face must hide what the false heart doth know.

The assassination takes place. And before Brutus meets his own death, on the point of his own sword, he experiences – though less fully than Macbeth – the realisation of horror. War has come. Brutus is in his tent, at night. And the ghost of Caesar enters.

Brutus: How ill this taper burns. Ha! who comes here?
I think it is the weakness of mine eyes
That shapes this monstrous apparition.
It comes upon me. Art thou anything?
Art thou some god, some angel, or some devil,
That makest my blood cold, and my hair to stare?
Speak to me what thou art.
Ghost: Thy evil spirit, Brutus.

17

It is not a weak spirit, either; and as the disasters multiply around him, Brutus exclaims:

O Julius Caesar, thou art mighty yet!
Thy spirit walks abroad, and turns our swords
In our own proper entrails.

The horror which Brutus here feels is to be traced directly to the original flaw in his soul. He had no confidence in the power of love, but he relied on death. And now, the love he did not trust is replaced by an evil spirit; and the death, in which he did repose his faith, is ineffectual.

This is one of the themes which runs through all Shakespeare's tragedies: to kill someone is never the way out. Killing cannot, according to Shakespeare, be a solution; because, in the final sense, killing is impossible. The ghost always comes back:

'Thou shalt see me at Philippi!' says Caesar's ghost.

'To-morrow in the battle think on me!' say the ghosts to Richard III.

And the ghost of Banquo quickly intrudes upon the feast of Macbeth's ambition. Shakespeare believes in immortality, and draws the logical conclusion: whatever may be the outcome of killing one's enemies, one thing it can never be is a conclusive victory.

3

Hamlet: Choosing

B RUTUS, we are told, 'was Caesar's angel'. Desdemona was Othello's love. Duncan was Macbeth's king, who had lately done him honour. Each of the three assassins was striking at his own good. He was striking at himself. And it is Shakespeare's purpose to show that from the moment of the deed his own life withers, and gradually goes down to dusty death. Their action is condemned with a general comment, 'It is not, and it cannot come to good.'

The case of Hamlet, however, is far more difficult. He had as good reason to hate his uncle as anyone could have. And it is the verdict of almost every reader and critic that since Claudius deserved punishment, and since no one but Hamlet could bring him to book, it was his duty to do so. There is wide agreement that Hamlet's failure does not lie in his doing the deed, but in his delay. To think otherwise is to give up human law.

But if the ethical implications of Shakespeare's tragic sequence hold good in *Hamlet*, as they do in his other tragedies, then he must think otherwise; because in every other instance he shows the tragic outcome to result from a series of wrong actions done by the hero. If Shakespeare

believed that it was Hamlet's duty to take revenge, then
the play stands out as a solitary exception to all the rest.
This, to say the least, is unlikely; and when we measure
Hamlet by the pattern, and consider its themes in the
widest context of Shakespearean thought – especially in
relation to *Measure for Measure*, which was probably written directly after – then we see it is impossible. Shakespeare, of course, was well aware of how momentous such
a reversal of the common judgment is; and it is partly for
that reason that he leaves it for us to draw the inference.
When we do, *Hamlet* becomes invested with a new
grandeur: it is a great challenge – as the Gospels are a
great challenge – to all our preconceptions of what justice
really is.

A key to Hamlet, one of several, is in Ophelia's exclam-
ation:

O, what a noble mind is here o'erthrown!

It is true that he was pretending to be mad when she said
that; but it is nevertheless appropriate to his real state
throughout the play. So great was the overthrow of his
mind that it was matched with a longing that life itself
should be overthrown:

            ... to die, to sleep,
No more; and by a sleep to say we end
The heart-ache and the thousand natural shocks
That flesh is heir to, 'tis a consummation
Devoutly to be wished. To die ...

Could any man be more overthrown, and still live? Ophelia's words are true of Hamlet's real state throughout the
tragedy.

Why was Hamlet overthrown? He was sickened, of course, by what was going on around him. Too much was rotten in the state of Denmark, and it came too close – his father, his uncle, his mother. He saw the world as an unweeded garden. But all that, bad though it was, is only a setting. The overthrow is within.

When Hamlet hears the facts from the ghost, he immediately commits himself to take revenge. This is the first reaction of his character. Then he reflects. The taking of revenge requires an act of blood; and Hamlet finds – as Macbeth and Brutus did – that there is a quality within him, his own 'proper self', which opposes the killing. I will substantiate this point later; but if it be granted for the present moment, we see Hamlet's situation, and Shakespeare's intention, in a flash. A noble nature is committed to an ignoble act. It is a contradiction in terms. Hamlet cannot sweep to his revenge until his nobility has been overthrown. Before the play opens, he had his nobility: when it ends, he has his revenge. And all that lies between is his progressive overthrow, the gradual disowning of his higher self. He dies with several crimes upon his hands.

This situation, if accepted in those terms, involves more than Hamlet's downfall; it means the rejection of conventional standards of justice. Shakespeare did accept it in this way. And faced with the choice, nobility or revenge, he unequivocally decided for nobility. But this implies a new ethical code, to the elaboration of which his later plays are devoted. If we throw out retributive justice, what can we put in its place? His answer is, creative mercy. This becomes a swelling theme with Shakespeare, and is briefly put in the lines from *Cymbeline*:

Kneel not to me:
The power that I have on you is to spare you;
The malice towards you to forgive you. Live!
And deal with others better.

Of this act of creative mercy we might reverse the general comment on the tragedies and say, 'It is, and it needs must come to good.' But Hamlet's misfortune is to have been so close to this position, and yet to have fallen short – 'The little less, what worlds away!'

I will now return to the point that Hamlet was so near to Shakespeare's higher standard that he inwardly condemned the one to which he had bound himself. It is a striking thing about Shakespeare's tragic characters that they know, deep down, what they ought to do. They frequently give themselves and one another the right advice – but they fail to take it. What then, in Shakespeare's opinion, ought Hamlet to have done? He should have acted on the advice Polonius gave to Laertes. There is a special reason why this advice was given to Laertes which I will touch on later; but it states a principle which, as we shall see, Hamlet fully acknowledged.

As these lines are possibly the hardest-worked quotation from the whole of Shakespeare, there is a danger that they may slip from our minds as easily as they slip from our tongues. They need emphasizing, not because they are recondite, but because they are too familiar. They are basic to Shakespeare's philosophy; and he repeats the principle they embody many times in the plays and the sonnets. 'I am that I am.' And to that – the highest I have yet found in myself – I must be true. The law we live by is within ourselves, and not outside:

This above all: to thine own self be true,
And it must follow, as the night the day,
Thou canst not then be false to any man.
Farewell: my blessing season this in thee!

The last line is Shakespeare's valediction to Everyman.

This was also Hamlet's standard. And at a moment when Polonius seems inclined to forget his own advice, Hamlet reminds him of it. They are discussing the players, Polonius says that he will treat them according to their deserts. And Hamlet at once replies, with a sudden flash of his true nobility, No, better!

Use every man after his desert, and who should 'scape whipping. Use them after your own honour and dignity.

It is the same thing as being true to oneself. Hamlet knew that he should treat others according to his own standard, and not descend – when it would be descent – to theirs. But what was Hamlet's one-time standard of human dignity? He tells us, in these words:

What a piece of work is a man! how noble in reason! how infinite in faculty! in form, in moving, how express and admirable! in action how like an angel! in apprehension how like a god! the beauty of the world!

Hamlet is not quoting poetry, he is describing the former vision of his own soul. Ophelia was right: such visions come only to a noble mind. And a nobility so compounded is incompatible with blood revenge. One or the other must go. And that is why Hamlet wavers.

I said that all Shakespeare's tragedies stem from a temptation. How does this apply to Hamlet? His tempter was his father's ghost. It was an evil counsellor to Hamlet, and led him to destruction. But was it an honest ghost? Yes and no. The majesty of buried Denmark, armed, cap-à-pie in complete steel, represents the old law – an eye for an eye, a tooth for a tooth – which is justice of a sort. But it was wrong for Hamlet; because, in his soul, the new law of creative mercy had already been conceived; but, for his tragedy, it was still-born.

4

Hamlet:
Stepping into Darkness

ALTHOUGH *Hamlet* was written before *Macbeth* and *Othello*, nevertheless, from the ethical point of view, it represents the last analysis of tragedy. *Macbeth* and *Othello* show that crime leads to tragedy, about which there is no debate; *Hamlet* shows that a code of conduct which is consistent with conventional law may do the same. Shakespeare was not willing to come to rest on this grim conclusion, and he was also no anarchist; logic, therefore, drove him to a new conception of law. In this sense, *Hamlet* is a turning-point; and accordingly we must examine its construction more closely.

At the opening of the play – as in other tragic openings – Shakespeare discloses to us the character of the 'voice', in this case the ghost, which will later speak in the temptation. When the first scene closes, we can be definitely sure, by comparison with Shakespeare's methods in other plays, that whatever the promptings or suggestions the ghost may make, when the temptation comes, they will lead to evil, and to the downgoing path towards the tragic act.

When the cock crows, the ghost starts, 'like a guilty thing upon a fearful summons'. It cannot stand the presence of 'the god of day'. That, from Shakespeare, is very suspicious. But he clinches it beyond a doubt in the next speech. During the season of Christ's birth, Marcellus tells us, such spirits cannot walk at all, and 'the nights are wholesome'. Surprisingly little in Shakespeare is superfluous, and he is not here giving us some unnecessary folklore. He is saying that the principle which the ghost stands for is incompatible with the law of love and mercy, symbolised by the birth of Christ.

The nature of the tempter having been established, we now consider – as in other plays – the state of soul of the person to be tempted. Why is Hamlet ripe for this particular temptation?

Hamlet is first shown to us not in natural sorrow but in embittered melancholy, and this is a debilitating state of mind. But to counterbalance this – and throughout the play there is a continual weighing of opposites – he is aware of 'that within which passeth show'. The reason for his melancholy, in the broadest terms, is that the world where he must live falls too far below the standard of his ideals. His metaphor, 'Hyperion to a satyr', is not merely a contrast between two people, but also between bright vision and muddy fact. Many people are in a somewhat similar situation. To pass beyond it, they must make a choice. They may attempt, however small the achievement, to transmute the base world to the ideal; or they may give up the higher standard and deal with the lower world by its own age-old methods. Briefly, when they emerge from inactivity, they must either rise to the new law or revert to the old. And in Shakespeare it is in the temptation scenes that they are forced to choose.

The fact that Hamlet had already begun to romanticise his father and to hate his uncle reveals to us his most vulnerable point. And in all his tragedies, Shakespeare shows us a temptation devilishly adapted to probe each hero's weakest spot. We know, already, where Hamlet will be predisposed to fall. And when the ghost speaks, Hamlet exclaims, 'O my prophetic soul! My uncle!' He was ripe to be tempted to that assassination.

The temptation scene now follows, according to Shakespeare's pattern; and every earlier intimation is confirmed. Shakespeare can make words so live that they seem to breathe, and the atmosphere that gathers round the ghost is an exhalation less of purgatory than of the pit. Certainly, the poor ghost is deserving of our pity; but it is clearly in no position to give good counsel.

Hamlet yields, and immediately he is plunged into the first inner conflict. In his previous soliloquy he was disgusted; in this, he is distracted:

> O all you host of Heaven! ...
> And shall I couple Hell?

Indeed he must. He is poised between them, and whatever move he makes will be towards one or the other. He vacillates, because he cannot do anything else. And his vacillations, with their accompanying conflict, continue throughout the play. But we may be sure, knowing Shakespeare's methods elsewhere, that he will slip gradually down, towards the tragic act, when we reach the line:

> Yea, from the table of my memory,
> I'll wipe away ...

all that was best there. We must not be misled by Hamlet's own adjective 'trivial'; it is a deliberate denigration, because the 'fond records' would have been on the side of light, and he is going to wipe them out. It is not an easy thing to do, but – 'I have sworn't!'

The revelation of that first inner conflict has put us in a position to prophesy. What is to come is already shaped in outline. A nature whose native inclination is to light has sworn itself to darkness. A tremendous spiritual battle must ensue. If darkness is to win – as it does – then certain forces of light must first be vanquished; and we are shown this taking place. We have already said that Hamlet's saving course, in Shakespeare's view, would have been fidelity to his own self. And as Hamlet knows this, the downward journey is very difficult. To proceed by calmly ignoring his ideal is impossible; it puts up resistance, and it has to be cast out. Nor is this all: he must also betray love.

Shakespeare presents love, in the sonnets, as the soul's guiding star (a view shared by many other poets, Dante in particular), and we may see from the line –

But bears it out even to the edge of doom

– how closely the ideas of love and fidelity are interwoven in his thought. Hamlet, before the play opens, shared this ideal of love; for he had once written to Ophelia, 'Doubt thou the stars are fire ... but never doubt I love ... I love thee best, O most best, believe it ... thine evermore ....'

Ophelia symbolises the love-star in Hamlet's soul – inspiring him, when he is moving upward; but an irksome reproach now that he has sworn to sink. And his rejection of her is the rejection of his guiding self. Admirers of

Hamlet have tended to veil his conduct towards Ophelia: Shakespeare, on the contrary, gives it prominence, showing it as a major symptom of the sickness of his soul. And following his frequent practice of casting the shadow before the substance, he gives us, as well as Ophelia, a warning of what is to come in her first scene. Her brother says to her:

> Perhaps he loves you now;
> And now no soil nor cautel doth besmirch
> The virtue of his will: but you must fear,
> His greatness weigh'd, his will is not his own ...

There is more in this, for us, than a reference to Hamlet's position as a prince. Shakespeare is always fond of writing in double meanings, and these words are a statement and a prophecy: Hamlet loves Ophelia now, because the virtue of his will has not been besmirched and soiled, yet; but in the very next scene he meets the ghost; and after that his will is not his own. Having yielded to the temptation, his true self is no longer in command, as according to Shakespeare's ethic it always should be; he is thereafter in the position of Brutus, plunged into the phantasma and the hideous dream, in which it is the Genius – an evil Genius – that controls his mortal instruments and not the pristine virtue of his will. He is about to make the terrible promise, the dire nature of which few readers fully grasp:

> And thy commandment all alone shall live,
> Within the book and volume of my brain ...

This oath is mind-shattering. If kept, it can only lead to madness; and having taken it, it is impossible, in Shakespeare's own judgment, impossible for him to remain true to love – love and the oath are mutually exclusive. All this is just about to take place; and in his warning speech, Laertes is allowed to prophesy:

> Contagious blastments are most imminent.
> Fear it, Ophelia, fear it ...

Well she may; since it will break her heart, overthrow her reason and bring her to the grave. It is fatal to our understanding of the play if the pity and pardon we may grant to Hamlet himself leads us to condone, or even to extenuate, the real evil of his acts; because it is a principle with Shakespeare that if the hero's actions are right, the tragic ending does not take place. We shall examine this principle where he works it out in detail, in *Measure for Measure*, *The Winter's Tale* and *The Tempest*. Much has been said, and rightly, about the artistic unity of *Hamlet*; but there is a wider consideration to which full weight has not been given, and that is the ethical unity of Shakespeare's work as a whole. In point of fact, Shakespeare gives this precedence over the artistic unity of any particular play, and it may serve as a lantern to the critic in many a dark passage.

Before trying to throw light on Hamlet's relations with Ophelia, there is one misconception I should like to remove. Hamlet's apologists have alleged that she 'jilted him'. He himself could not have looked on it in that light. They were not betrothed; and in their time a girl had not the freedom to flirt that a modern girl has. To an Elizabethan audience (as to a Latin one to-day) it would have seemed the plain duty of a father to keep his daughter away from a young man who was making clandestine love to her and might have seduced her; and it would have been her duty, in spite of heart-break, to obey. Hamlet

could not have misunderstood that, and there is nothing
in the play to suggest that he did. If he had intended marriage, he would have approached Polonius; and if he did
not, then the father's conduct was strictly in accordance
with convention. What prevented Hamlet from marrying
Ophelia? Clearly, she loved him, and would have con-
sented. The queen wished it, and says so, 'I hoped thou
shouldst have been my Hamlet's wife.' The king would
not have objected. Polonius would have been overjoyed;
what better match could his daughter have made? Then
why were they not, at least, betrothed? Because Hamlet
never asked her. And therefore, surely, it is mistaken to
talk of his being jilted. He did not think he was; he, the
heir apparent, the most eligible bachelor in Denmark,
knew that Ophelia could have been his wife for the asking. He did not ask. And it was not her fault, nor her
father's, that his behaviour to her was abominable. The
reason, and it is important to discover it, was in himself.

The entry of Ophelia raises a point of much importance
with regard to Shakespeare's technique. This will be
explained later, but it must here be mentioned. Shakespeare was much influenced by the allegorical tradition
elaborated in the poetry of the Middle Ages. And he
makes more use of it than some of his commentators
recognise. To him it was still fresh and alive; to us it may
seem stale, not in itself, but because we are divided from
it by a period of debased allegory, like a pile of wilting
flowers on a grave. Debased allegory is to that of medieval
poetry as Victorian Gothic is to Chartres.

In strict derivation, allegory means other-speak. Double-
talk, one might be tempted to call it; and Shakespeare,
like the poets of the Middle Ages, delights in subtle

double-talk. In our own century we are unattuned to poetic allegory, and may think of allegorical figures as puppetry. There is a penalty for this: we sometimes fail to see allegory, unless it is so crude as to be a blemish, or unless a label, 'This work is allegorical', has already been tied on.

To Shakespeare, allegory is not puppetry, but a deeper level of life; and he uses it frequently, where we are liable to miss it, in order that we may actually see the inner drama of his heroes' souls. This is one of the most significant elements of his art; and if it eludes us, we are losing his deepest thoughts. But it is easy for us to miss, partly because we are out of sympathy with it, and partly because Shakespeare uses it with great subtlety.

Many of his characters are dual: they are human beings and allegorical figures at the same time. And if we are not alerted to this, we may see nothing but the human being. When we try to analyse, completely, a Shakespearean character by psychological means, we run into trouble; because the allegorical aspect will not yield to this interpretation. Scenes, too, that are psychologically baffling, may be allegorically lucid; and when so considered, they fall into place.

Ophelia is a dual character of this kind: she is the girl we all know, and she is also an allegorical figure representing a quality in Hamlet's soul. When Hamlet speaks to her, he is sometimes talking to a girl, sometimes to an entity in himself, and often to both. As an allegorical figure, she is that point of love in Hamlet which is the centre of his true nobility; and therefore she coincides with his highest self, which he is about to fail, and is a symbol of the law of love, to which he cannot rise. Everything that happens to Ophelia is an allegory of what is taking place in Hamlet.

When he treated her – we know he once did – as a lover should treat his beloved, he was noble and could have been false to no man. When he has sworn to take revenge, but cannot do so until love has been cast out, we have those poignant scenes between them, when he is driving love from his soul and at the same time breaking her heart. When his nobility totters, she goes mad; when it is a ruin, she is drowned. If we fail to see that Ophelia – and many other characters in Shakespeare – are dual, and that one half of them is a carefully created allegorical figure, then we not only miss much of Shakespeare's meaning, but we are deprived of the pleasure of appreciating one of the exquisite qualities of his art.

When Hamlet sees Ophelia, he is confronting his better self. And the first meeting between them, after his first temptation, is a farewell. This is how Ophelia describes it:

> He raised a sigh so piteous and profound
> That it did seem to shatter all his bulk
> And end his being: that done, he lets me go;
> And with his head over his shoulder turn'd,
> He seem'd to find his way without his eyes;
> For out o'doors he went without their help,
> And to the last, bended their light on me.

Shatter – end his being – lets me go – way without eyes: not a word without a second meaning. And Polonius draws the correct inference, allegorically, when he says that Hamlet has gone mad because he has lost access to Ophelia. But Hamlet himself, we must remember, was to blame for that, because his love-making was equivocal.

33

After his great soliloquy, 'To be, or not to be...', in which he gives expression to his longing for death, there follows a dialogue with Ophelia which is really a continuation of the death theme; indeed, it is more, it is part of the long-drawn act of spiritual suicide. It may be understood as a pitiful meditation within a soul bent upon self-destruction, and denying its own saving quality of beauty and love. And that same quality is reminding him of his own gifts and his own self:

O help him, you sweet Heavens!

Throughout the long soliloquy, every idea is negative. To live is to 'bear the whips and scorns of time', to die is to fly to other ills 'we know not of'. Even the possibility of joy is excluded; and that brings Hamlet near to the darkness of Macbeth; for when life loses joy, it also loses meaning. Then, for a moment, a light is struck:

Soft you now, the fair Ophelia!

She reminds him of his former gifts, 'I pray you, now receive them.' She is not throwing them back in his face. Why should she? She loves him, and her father is no longer opposed. Can anyone doubt what she is longing for? Clearly, she is trying to reawaken his nobility by the sight of these remembrances of love. It is, almost, his last chance. But Hamlet is as determined as Othello to put out the light, and he answers, 'I never gave you aught.' In under-meaning, this denial is akin to that made by St Peter.

All of this dialogue may be taken in two ways: a man tormenting the girl who loves him; and a soul poised and struggling between heaven and hell. It is sometimes said that the downward path is easy; it is not. Love must be fended off at every step. And to do this it is helpful – as Hamlet here shows – to persuade oneself that love is a harlot. In what follows, he virtually calls her that, and nunnery is probably to be taken in its coarse second meaning; for her degradation would remove the chief obstacle in his tragic path. As he leaves her, he says again:

To a nunnery, go!

He has cast love out. And Ophelia's next lines tell us the cost, to himself, of doing so:

O, what a noble mind is here o'erthrown!
     ... that noble and most sovereign reason,
Like sweet bells jangled, out of tune and harsh;
That unmatch'd form and feature of blown youth
Blasted with ecstasy: O! woe is me,
To have seen what I have seen, see what I see!

Many critics have been puzzled by Hamlet's treatment of Ophelia. Dover Wilson, for example, writes: 'that Shakespeare intended us to interpret Hamlet's speeches here, together with some of those in the nunnery scene, as, like Othello's, belonging to the brothel is, I think, incontestible.' If we accept Hamlet as a gentleman and Ophelia as an innocent girl who loves him – matters which no one doubts – then there is no psychological explanation that carries conviction. And there is certainly no explanation in terms of our conceptions of the theatre; for, to quote Dover Wilson again, 'it endangers the very life of the play'. This is one of those situations – and there are many in Shakespeare – where psychological analysis lets us down; but allegorical analysis not only explains what is taking place but shows it to be inevitable. It is not enough to ask ourselves, as the Victorian critics did, What is the *character* of Ophelia? The question is, What is the *significance* of Ophelia? And that includes both character, in the psychological sense, and allegory. Many related things stand in the way of Hamlet's oath of vengeance – nobility, love, reason, and even, at the last, life; that is why the inner conflict is so bitter and prolonged. A coarse nature would have overthrown them quickly, an enlightened one would have behaved like Prospero. Hamlet stands between. He sinks into the quicksand inch by inch. And this protracted death is shown to us, in several places, allegorically.

The effort – indeed the necessity – to degrade the law of love in Ophelia's person, by equating love with harlotry, is paralleled by the building of a preposterously romantic fantasy around the law of revenge, as personified by the late king. This, in his mind's eye, has become Hamlet's picture of his father:

> See, what a grace was seated on this brow;
> Hyperion's curls, the front of Jove himself,
> An eye like Mars, to threaten and command,
> A station like the herald Mercury ...

It is romantic nonsense. What was the truth of the elder Hamlet?

> I am thy father's spirit,
> Doomed for a certain term to walk the night,
> And for the day confin'd to fast in fires,
> Till the foul crimes done in my days of nature
> Are burnt and purg'd away. But that I am forbid
> To tell the secrets of my prison-house,

I could a tale unfold whose lightest word
Would harrow up thy soul ...

Those are the ' facts', from the one witness who was in a position to know them. And Shakespeare means us to infer that, morally speaking, there was little to choose between the late king and the living one. Their 'foul crimes' were different, but their balance of sin was much the same. Nor was either of them devoid of good qualities. But Hamlet can only proceed by reversing his values; Ophelia is a near harlot, and his father is a near god. He must persuade himself that 'fair is foul and foul is fair'; it is a part of his overthrow – part of all tragic overthrows – and by the fifth act the reversal is complete, and he reaches the point where it is 'conscience' that pricks him on to crime.

Hamlet is so fully successful in hypnotizing himself that he partially hypnotises the audience as well. We have to pinch ourselves awake in order not to accept his valuation of the other characters. It is an hallucination – like the third-act appearance of the ghost, which was then visible to himself alone. Claudius and the queen were certainly bad enough; but they were a great deal better than Hamlet paints them; and Shakespeare means us to estimate their characters not by what Hamlet says but by what they do – much of which is creditable.

After the dismissal of Ophelia, we have reached a point when – by analogy with other tragedies – we should expect a second temptation and an intensification of the inner conflict. Does this apply to Hamlet?

I think it does, but in a special way. After the first temptation, Hamlet administered the tragic oath to himself,

'I have sworn't!' And thereafter he becomes his own tempter. The scene following his dialogue with Ophelia is the play-within-the-play. It was Hamlet, of course, who adapted this play; and in one of its undermeanings it is a pouring of poison into his own ear. The loathsome skin-disease, there described as the consequence of the poison, reflects also the condition of a soul which has become so sick that it now sees the universe as 'no other thing to me, than a foul and pestilent congregation of vapours'.

In the play-scene, the poison-in-the-ear theme, which was first announced by the ghost, is fully expanded and acted out. It is thus a repetition of the first temptation, but much more vividly presented, and constitutes a second. Immediately, the inner conflict flares up, like flames on a freshly stoked fire. There is the universal cry:

Lights! lights! lights!

This is most important. When Shakespeare lays special stress on light, he is using it symbolically. He is telling us that at this moment there is a dire need for spiritual light; and it would probably have been in the prayer scene, which follows, if he had been intending to show us a res-olution of tragedy, which we shall examine later, that he would have turned the course of events. But the condi-tions for a resolution are not fulfilled, and we are therefore precipitated towards the deadly outcome. All the charac-ters fail at this point in some degree, but chiefly Hamlet. It is particularly to be noticed that just when the king – and to some extent the queen – is making a genuine movement towards light, Hamlet makes a corresponding movement into darkness. Critics who are determined to see the king – as Shakespeare did not draw him – without redeeming qualities, minimise this; but Shakespeare's characters are always sincere in their asides and soliloquies. In his earlier aside —

> How smart a lash that speech doth give my conscience!
> Oh heavy burden!

— we are meant to see a sinner whose redemption is by no means impossible. The cry for light comes from his heart; and in his prayer he only just falls short. The pity and horror of it is that at this crucial juncture Hamlet plunges downward. When the king leaves the stage calling for light, and in the next scene will be on his knees to God, Hamlet speaks the dreadful soliloquy, which is virtually an invitation to the devil:

> ... hell itself breathes out
> Contagion to this world: now I could drink hot blood,
> And do such bitter business as the day
> Would quake to look on.

After that, it is impossible to lift the action to the level on which a resolution could have been achieved. Within minutes we reach the point of no return. Polonius has been killed by Hamlet — the 'hot blood' has been drunk. Hamlet has himself killed a father, and is about to become the object of an avenging son. In Laertes he has a deadly twin.

The fact that the killing of Polonius is a turning point is accentuated by its allegorical significance. Like Ophelia, Polonius is a double character. Shakespeare has several such ancient counsellors — Gonzalo, in *The Tempest*, for one — and they have a quality in common, they are all faithful. Shakespeare pokes plenty of kindly fun at these old men, and they are useful stage characters, but he respects, them, and they share one of his most cherished mottos:

I will be true, despite thy scythe and thee.

In a sense, they are all expressions of a single figure – Fidelity. Polonius shows us this second nature when he says:

I hold my duty as I hold my soul
Both to my God, and to my gracious king.

This is confirmed when the king gives him the character:

As of a man faithful and honourable.

And Shakespeare confirms it by making him the mouthpiece of his cardinal point of conduct:

To thine own self be true.

Fidelity to the higher standard is one of the qualities that Hamlet must be rid of before he can take revenge. He is therefore continually trying to shake Polonius off, and to denigrate him in words so as to discredit him within himself. 'These tedious old fools.' 'If like a crab you could go backward', he tells Polonius, you would be like me: a neat description of his own retreat. But he can never forget that Polonius is the father of Ophelia – that Fidelity goes with Love. And therefore he degrades them in his own mind and speech (for instance, in the coarse under-meaning of the 'fishmonger' scene) into a bawd and his harlot.

But he must be rid of both, father and daughter, before he can keep his oath to darkness. Fidelity must die first; and therefore Polonius is stabbed behind the arras. Fidelity is killed behind the dark veils of Hamlet's soul. This is a point of no return. We should expect a swift decline. And that, in reality, is what we get; but in a curiously masked manner.

Early in the fourth act Hamlet steps out of the play. He does not return to it until the graveyard scene, at the beginning of the fifth act. On first thoughts it seems odd to lose the chief character for so long, and just at the moment when the action should be moving faster. Partial explanations can be easily found; but it is only explained in full if we see that Shakespeare is laying particular stress on the allegorical construction at this point. Hamlet steps out on the line:

> From this time forth,
> My thoughts be bloody or be nothing worth.

He has killed fidelity to the higher standard, and he has discarded love; but that does not mean that his soul is empty. When the angels leave, the demons come in. Where Fidelity and Love had been, unbounded Revenge has replaced them. And Shakespeare sets this before us, incarnate on the stage, in another dual character – Laertes.

It is not coincidence that – in the first act – Laertes went to study sword-play in France on the very day that Hamlet began to study vengeance; and that both are perfected, or nearly so, together; nor that Hamlet says, in the last act, 'Since he went into France, I have been in continual practice.' Nor is it chance that Polonius and Ophelia were, or tried to be, a good influence on both, and that all barriers to vengeance are down now that Polonius is dead and Ophelia mad. Such converging lines are never accidental in Shakespeare; they are carefully drawn into the allegorical pattern.

41

Laertes is not only the man we see on the stage; he is also an allegorical figure of the *new* content of Hamlet's soul – uninhibited vengeance. So we may say that Hamlet has not left the play: when Ophelia and Laertes are on stage, only Hamlet's body is missing, and we watch what is happening within him.

Ophelia enters first. She is out of her mind, and singing. The song is not really about her father; it has all to do with the betrayal and death of true love – of herself and of Hamlet's self.

> Which bewept to the grave did go
> With true-love showers.

Then we have the inrush of Laertes: Hamlet's vengeance incarnate. Why should the people call for Laertes to be king, when Hamlet, we have been told, is a popular favourite and the rightful heir? It is one of many hints to us that Laertes is now to be seen as an aspect of Hamlet. It is against the king that Laertes and the mob first clamour for revenge, just as Hamlet is doing within himself. And Laertes' ranting speech

> That drop of blood that's calm proclaims me bastard,
> Cries cuckold to my father, brands the harlot
> Even here, between the chaste unsmirched brows
> Of my true mother.

is a shouting in public of much that is in Hamlet's mind, of several references to his mother, and of the rant of his soliloquy:

> ... bloody, bawdy villain,
> Remorseless, treacherous, lecherous, kindless villain!
> O Vengeance!

This content of Hamlet's soul is being objectified. And then, gradually, the vengeance is turned on to Hamlet himself. The evil in a man's soul hits back at him, both as a demon within and as a being of flesh and blood. If we overlook the allegory in this act, we fail to see Shakespeare's profoundest intention; and we also lose the opportunity of appreciating a wonderfully adroit piece of allegorical construction.

The mad Ophelia now returns for her last scene: 'There's rosemary, that's for remembrance. Pray, love, remember.' There is no trace of bitterness in her, hers is pure love to the end:

> And will he not come again?
> And will he not come again?
> No, no, he is dead;
> Go to thy death-bed,
> He never will come again.

It is not for the loss of a father, but of a lover, that love dies. So she prays for mercy upon every soul, and wanders away to drown. The best part of Hamlet is dead: he is alone with the Furies. The king now speaks to Laertes thus:

> Hamlet comes back. What would you undertake
> To show yourself your father's son in deed
> More than in words?
> *Laertes:* To cut his throat i'the church.
> *King:* No place, indeed, should murder sancturise;
> Revenge should have no bounds.

Hamlet, the son avenging a father, is now to have a father's death avenged upon him by a son. When fidelity and love are dead, revenge, indeed, has no bounds. And those who seek it get more of it than they wish.

Hamlet returns. And we have the scene in the church-yard where he and Laertes fight, though not yet to the death, in Ophelia's grave. Considered realistically, this scene offends against Shakespeare's own canon, 'That you o'erstep not the modesty of nature.' But, allegorically, it is a master-stroke. Love's grave is not a place of quiet death. As love withers and dies, hate grows and thrives. And as Hamlet leaps into the grave of his own love, the fingers of hate close round his throat:

> The devil take thy soul!

Here, Shakespeare himself is leading us close to the heart of Hamlet's mystery; and at the same time he is making an assertion that he reiterates in other plays: a soul that makes itself the grave of love inevitably becomes the womb of hate.

Even in the last scene of the last act, however, there is a brief flash of hope that the uttermost calamity might have been something less. Before they fight to what proves to be the death, Hamlet has asked pardon, and Laertes replies:

> I am satisfied in nature,
> Whose motive, in this case, should stir me most
> To my revenge; but in my terms of honour
> I stand aloof, and will no reconcilement,
> Till by some elder masters of known honour
> I have a voice and precedent for peace ...

This is a last betrayal of the standard of truth 'to thine own self'. Had he been true 'above all' to that, there would have been a reconciliation; but instead of maintaining his own standard 'in nature', he reverts to conventional judgments, and hands over the rulership of his own soul to 'elder masters' and their precedents – that is, to the ghost. Again, he is shown up as Hamlet's deadly twin.

We can now look back and see how allegorically apt is the scene in the first act between Polonius and Laertes. Fidelity is warning young revenge, which is just about to begin its studies in the rapier play of death. And from whom did Laertes learn this art? He tells the king, in the fourth act. It was from a Norman, 'gem of all the nation' of whose name there are variants – the Quarto of 1604 gives Lamord, the Folio of 1623, Lamound. Shakespeare is so careful to dot his i's and cross his t's that I have no doubt he wrote the first, and with grim intention – *la mort*!

Shakespeare's plays are – at the least – three things: magical poetry, excellent theatre, and ethical theorems of Euclidean logicality. The importance of the allegorical figures goes much beyond the interpretation of any particular play, because similar figures come back in other plays like 'redressings of a former sight'. There is nothing haphazard in their use. Their consistency springs from the fact that Shakespeare is making them express his own ethic; and when we isolate the allegorical structure from the 'trappings and the suits', we find a theorem in ethics. And gradually we may uncover a pattern which will be that of Shakespeare's own beliefs. These are not by any means familiar threadbare dogmas: in part, they seem to be metal smelted from the ore of life in the furnace of his own soul; in part, they are a syncretistic philosophy. This might represent the philosophy of a circle of Elizabethan thinkers who dared not express it openly for fear of the law. The Reformation did not, in itself, make unorthodoxy in religious matters safe.

In brief outline, the allegorical pattern of *Hamlet* is this: a soul that has risen almost to the point at which it will replace the law of the Old Testament by that of the New is tempted to revert to the ancient way, and yields. It swears the oath of vengeance. To keep the oath, it must first kill Fidelity to the higher law, and then cast out Love. It does so. But these are acts which also, under the old law, cry for vengeance. And, therefore, the outcome for that soul is that revenge is both inflicted and endured.

And this, Shakespeare maintains, is the state of man, until he is able to see and live by a higher standard. It is a state of self-slaughter on a racial scale, as is pointed by the play's last words:

Go, bid the soldiers shoot!

But against it an everlasting canon has been fixed.

5

Hamlet: Tragic Climax

W E HAVE SEEN that in other tragedies there is a realisation of horror, between the tragic act and the hero's death, which is directly related to the original flaw in his soul. Hamlet dies too quickly for this to happen in his own consciousness; but his special horror is revealed unsparingly to us.

The fourth act has shown us, allegorically, the disintegration of Hamlet's higher self in the drowning of Ophelia; and the full development of his revenge daemon in Laertes, pupil of Lamord, who returns for a mock 'crowning'. Hamlet's death-wish has triumphed over his love-wish. He comes back changed, because the tragic inversion has taken place. And when the fifth act opens, we find him in a setting which is really a materialisation of his new inner landscape – a graveyard.

Critics who think they see signs of regeneration in the course of *Hamlet* are ignoring the symbolic indications that Shakespeare gives. *Hamlet* is a study in degeneration from first to last, and that is the tragedy. If it be objected that some notion of regeneration is an integral part of our idea of tragedy, then it must be confessed that Shakespeare never wrote a tragedy of this ideal type; he wrote death-plays and birth-plays, and *Hamlet* is a death-play.

Lose not thy rights; nor, downward hurled and falling to the depths, plunge to the waters of black Acheron.

The loss of the soul's rights, and the resultant downward plunge, is almost a definition of Shakespearean tragedy. The stage conception of Hamlet as a princely philosopher, weak and irresolute at the outset, but strong and regenerate at the end, is the diametrical opposite of Shakespeare's meaning: a noble mind falling to Acheron is the dreadful spectacle we were intended to behold. Hamlet's spiritual apogee is expressed in his magnificent speech on the nature of man, which reflects his own pristine nobility; and if we set that against the bleeding bodies on which the curtain falls, we have the true gradient of the play.

'Self-slaughter' is the initial theme of his first soliloquy. This, coming at the outset, is prophetic, and is another of the keys to *Hamlet*. It was an inclination before he was tempted; and from the moment he yielded to the first temptation, self-slaughter is what he is doing throughout the play. But his is not the simple act of destroying the body, which is a short-lived thing at best; Hamlet's self-slaughter is incomparably more terrible: it is the slow killing of the higher qualities of his soul.

The realisation of horror is for us, as we watch his light gradually turning into darkness and his sense of value being inverted. But this should come as no surprise. We have been fully prepared for it. Hamlet's callous speech about the dead Polonius is not good theatre, but it is good allegory; because a king making a progress through the guts of a beggar is an apt, if disgusting, image of the debasement of sovereignty in himself. 'Hamlet', writes Tillyard, 'lacks a complication and an enrichment common in much tragedy: that of being to some extent, even a tiny extent, responsible for his misfortunes.' But this begs a question. Hamlet disavows the law of Christ to follow the law of Moses; and this, in a Christian, is sin. To reply that most Christians do the same is true but unhelpful; of course they do, that is why there are so many corpses when the last curtain falls.

In speech after speech we see that Hamlet is increasingly taking black for white. The war expedition of Fortinbras, which Shakespeare paints as criminal lunacy, appears to him as an example of virtue. 'Rightly to be great,' he assures himself, is not to act in a good cause, but 'greatly to find quarrel in a straw ...', and to risk the lives of an army 'even for an egg-shell'.

> ... to my shame I see
> The imminent death of twenty thousand men,
> That for a fantasy and trick of fame
> Go to their graves like beds ...

> O, from this time forth,
> My thoughts be bloody, or be nothing worth!

Fortinbras is no hero to Shakespeare, but he has become one to Hamlet.

Almost everything Hamlet says in the fifth act – and much that is said by others – reveals this inversion of his standard. We remember that once he saw man as 'the beauty of the world'. Now, he sees every high quality turned to its corresponding baseness, and harps on the theme that life, so far from having a flowering beyond death, is only a progress to worms and dust. When he speaks in terms of light, he applies them to the uses of darkness. So that his thought is close to that of Macbeth, for whom fair became foul, and life without signification. It is the consequence of the self-slaughter of his soul.

He looks at the skulls in the graveyard, and imagines that one belonged to a politician 'that would circumvent God'. Another to a courtier, whose praising was really begging. Another to a lawyer, whose present condition is 'the fine of his fines'. 'Here's a fine revolution' – in himself – if he had the trick to see it. The grave-maker sees it; and when Hamlet accuses him of lying, since graves are for the dead and not the quick, he replies: ' 'Tis a quick lie, sir. 'Twill away again from me to you.' Hamlet picks up the skull of the jester, reflects on it in terms of an excellence irrevocably lost, and lets it fall with the advice that the last of its 'flashes of merriment' should be a cruel one.

Then comes his dispute with Laertes over Ophelia, and the empty rhetoric of his boasts of love. Hamlet, who has caused her death, demands, 'What wilt thou *do* for her?' And he answers his own question:

> Make Ossa like a wart! Nay an thou'lt mouth,
> I'll rant as well as thou.

Though he still makes use of the language of light, the effect of it, now, is to sugar the devil. 'There's a divinity,' he says, 'that shapes our ends ...' But how, we must notice, does he make use of the divine intervention on this occasion? He uses it to forge a document, which sends two men to sudden death, 'Not shriving-time allow'd.' And how does he seal it?

> Why, even in this was heaven ordinant.
> I had my father's signet in my purse ...

This mingling of divinity and heaven with trickery and unshriven death is the picturing of God as serving the devil. It is difficult, at times, not to allow Hamlet's self-deception to deceive us, and his admirers gloss over this point; but Shakespeare does not. Unshriven death, with the implication of damnation, is the devil's main business. And this is not the first time – we remember the king at prayer – that Hamlet has coldly determined to people hell. One might consider the plotting of damnation to be the ultimate in crime; and equally to attribute the opportunity for doing it to the ordering of heaven, is the ultimate in madness. In Shakespeare, always, crime and madness are linked; and they are bound together, logically, by the inversion of value, which he invariably displays in the hero before he commits the tragic act. When this has taken place, the hero has got rid of conscience, the chief barrier to crime, and which, according to Shakespeare, 'is born of love'. The tragic path, then, is clear, and Shakespeare has traced it for us time and again: first the hero is untrue to his own self, then he casts out love, then conscience is gone – or, rather, inverted – and the devil enters into him.

Hamlet has now reached this position. There is no regeneration in the last act. On the contrary, Hamlet says explicitly that the unshriven deaths are not on his conscience; then he goes further – to let the king live is to be damned, and to kill him is 'perfect conscience'. We know, and can prove it to the hilt, that Shakespeare's view of perfect conscience is the act of creative mercy. Therefore, by the permanent standard of his own ethic, Shakespeare has turned Hamlet morally upside-down. And he never relents to the end. Hamlet's fine talk is now meretricious.

And he seals this with his last words, as if with his 'father's signet':

> ... th'election lights
> On Fortinbras, he has my dying voice ...

What is Fortinbras to Shakespeare? He is the symbol of war by 'ambition puff'd', embarked upon for a plot of land 'which is not tomb enough and continent to hide the slain'; and such a war, to Shakespeare, means the self-slaughter of mankind. A theme of suicide, spiritual and racial, runs through the play. In the first act, Fortinbras is a threat. In the second, the danger from him is averted by right negotiation and the help of the old king of Norway; and Polonius is made the father of this good news. In the fourth act, there is a sinister reminder of Fortinbras, when he leads an army against Poland:

> ... to gain a little patch of ground
> That hath in it no profit but the name.

In the last act, as a result of Hamlet's revenge, Fortinbras takes all. To Shakespeare, his accession means the defeat of humanity and the perpetuation of genocide:

> Go, bid the soldiers shoot!

These are the last words of the tragedy, except for the stage directions which underline them: 'A dead march. Exeunt, bearing off the bodies: after which a peal of ordnance is shot off.'

It is the very rhythm of death. And in this final act, especially, Shakespeare is at pains to show that the play is a demonstration of ethics of universal application. There lives a Hamlet in everyone. The grave-maker clown, who began his grave-making on the day of Hamlet's birth, cracks a joke to make the groundlings laugh and the thoughtful weep. Hamlet has been sent to England, says the grave-digger, because he is mad. In England – and for England read the world – his madness will not be noticed, 'for there all the men are as mad as he'. But it is not a cheerful sort of madness; it is of the kind that keeps grave-diggers at their work and rings down the curtain on a stage littered with corpses.

Shakespeare had no liking for corpses. He was a man of refined sensibility and deep compassion. Nor is he aiming to provide his audience with a perverted pleasure from the sight of 'superfluous death'. The corpses are there because they are the outcome of madness, poison and the rapier's thrust, and because the law of retributive justice has strewn the earth with them for ages:

> ... give order that these bodies
> High on a stage be placed to the view;
> And let me speak to the yet unknowing world
> How these things came about ...

Shakespeare is returning to the theme of unwitting racial suicide:

> And, in this upshot, purposes mistook
> Fall'n on the inventors' heads ...

And he might well have added, with all the bitterness of Faust:

> *Das ist deine Welt! das heisst eine Welt!* *

But there have been many intimations in *Hamlet* that a better world is possible. And Shakespeare, although he had other tragedies to write, now turns to the problem of its attainment.

---

* 'That is your world! That's *called* a world!'

6

Measure for Measure: Resolving Tragedy

THE RESOLUTION of tragedy is a complex problem; and Shakespeare does not attempt to answer the whole of it in one play, but breaks it up into its component parts. Power is an ingredient of all of them: everyone has the power to undertake a course of action, of which the outcome may be tragic or the reverse. But power is more or less circumscribed; and in a man who has authority over others, it will have its widest scope. This is a part of the problem with which Shakespeare deals in *Measure for Measure*:

> Man, proud man,
> Drest in a little brief authority,
> Most ignorant of what he's most assured,
> His glassy essence, like an angry ape,
> Plays such fantastic tricks before high heaven
> As make the angels weep ...

Surely, however, the authorities may follow an alternative course – one that will cause the angels to rejoice? Shakespeare thought so, and he states the situation somewhat in this manner. There is much wickedness in the world, and those who have the power to act must take account of it.

There would seem to be three courses open to them: first, a strict punishment that is appropriate to the crime; second, an indulgent policy of *laissez-faire*; third, some curative treatment for evil, which may be called creative mercy. After *Hamlet*, the logical step in Shakespeare's ethical enquiry would be to contrast these three methods, and the results of each, in a single play; and in *Measure for Measure* this is what he does.

A full analysis of *Measure for Measure* would be a lengthy work, for the play is packed with meanings. But as we are only aiming, here, to trace the main line of development of Shakespeare's ethics, such detail is not necessary. It will be enough to consider its pattern, and to follow its more important themes.

First, as we saw, it contrasts three methods of dealing with offence: punishment, indulgence and regeneration.

Shakespeare has already dealt with punishment in other plays, and his conclusions here remain unaltered: if every man were given his strict deserts, all would be whipped and most beheaded. We need not discuss this theme again, except to notice that in *Measure for Measure* its cold logic, which was established in *Hamlet*, is given a religious warmth in the lines:

> How would you be
> If He, which is the top of judgment, should
> But judge you as you are? O, think on that;
> And mercy then will breathe within your lips,
> Like man new made.

So much for punishment: it is not conducive to the great ideal, which is 'man new made'. But indulgence, the obvious alternative, is also found to be impracticable, and the results of it are summed up in the duke's speech:

We have strict statutes and most biting laws,
The needful bits and curbs to headstrong steeds,
Which for this fourteen years we have let slip ...
        ... so our decrees,
Dead to infliction, to themselves are dead;
And liberty plucks justice by the nose;
The baby beats the nurse, and quite athwart
Goes all decorum.

We need not examine the many illustrations of this in
Measure for Measure, for the proposition is plainly true.
Shakespeare's new problem now stands in isolation. He is
to show, or begin to show, in what way creative mercy differs from mere indulgence, the one bringing regeneration,
while the other brings only chaos to society.

Such is the background: for the past fourteen years the
Duke of Vienna has been so lenient to his subjects, so spar-
ing in his application of the law's harsh penalties, that the
law itself is no longer feared and society is in confusion.
To remedy this the duke has two plans. One of these he
makes known at the outset; but his true plan is only
revealed gradually as the play unfolds.

His declared intention, the superficial one, is to hand
over the government of Vienna temporarily to a man of
spotless moral reputation, Angelo, who has no hesitation
in inflicting the rigour of the law. In theory, this ought to
restore society to a healthy condition. Meanwhile, the
duke is supposed to have gone away on a journey; but,
in reality, he disguises himself as a monk, and remains in
Vienna to carry out his deeper intention, which is to cure
his subjects instead of punishing them. We soon find that
we are watching, not simply a play, but an experiment in
psychiatry.

The duke, being Shakespeare, knows that Angelo's retributive justice, carried to its logical conclusion, will end as tragically as *Hamlet*. It will make a graveyard in the fifth act, and call that justice, as so many tragic heroes do. And the first step, of several, in what we may call the duke's treatment, is to let the tragedy almost happen; so that the main characters receive a severe awakening jolt, by being confronted with the prospect of death. To face them with death, and prepare them to meet it, is the duke's shock-therapy, and is the preliminary to helping them to discover their true selves. It is to make for them, as he explains it, 'heavenly comforts of despair'.

Angelo, therefore, assumes the government. According to an ancient statute, anyone who commits adultery is to be put to death. In the lax moral condition of the state, this would mean executing the majority; but a first example is to be made of Claudio. Claudio has had a love affair – which is represented as true and mutual love, although outside marriage – with Juliet. Juliet is with child, and Claudio is to die for it. It is not a question of general justice. Claudio is less guilty than most other characters in the play; but a warning example is to be made of him, so that 'justice' is itself being unjust:

> ... on whom it will, it will;
> On whom it will not, so ...

The next step in the ethical demonstration is to show that Angelo, the judge, is morally no better than Claudio, the condemned. And we may well think back to an inference we drew from *Hamlet*, that the accusing ghost only seemed to be morally superior to his usurping brother, their real sum of sin may have been much the same. In the present case, the judge is worse than the condemned.

The showing-up of Angelo is brought about by confronting him with his feminine counterpart, a woman of equal seeming saintliness, Isabella. Isabella is Claudio's sister. She is beautiful, conventionally virtuous, and cold; real humanity has never been awakened in her (although it will be); and when the play opens, she is on the verge of becoming a nun. She is asked by Lucio, a rakish friend of her brother, to intercede with Angelo. And somewhat reluctantly she agrees.

The scene which follows, between Isabella and Lucio on the one hand and Angelo on the other, is important for several reasons. We must unweave this tapestry and consider its main threads in isolation. First, we notice that what begins as an intercession for Claudio turns unexpectedly into a temptation for Angelo. Angelo, whom no woman has ever deeply stirred before, is overcome by a guilty desire for this snow-pure maiden, who is in many ways so like himself. Claudio has been condemned for fornication: Angelo, for the first time, is tempted to the same offence. But, as he himself has previously said:

'Tis one thing to be tempted, Escalus,
Another thing to fall.

What will the judge now do – live by the standard of the law he administers, or sink to the level of the man he has sentenced?

We know, of course, that he will sink, and sink lower than the man he has convicted; for that is part of the ethical theorem of the play. And in the light of Shakespeare's methods of construction in other plays, we can predict:

Angelo will have two temptations, followed by inner conflicts; he will commit the tragic act; he will realise its horror, and – Here comes the change from the tragic pattern. Because of the duke's intervention, because of his act of creative mercy – and for no other reason – the end will not be death. This brings us to the moral of the play: although every ingredient of tragedy may be present, a tragic climax may yet be averted by the power of love.

We will now briefly trace the tragic pattern as applied to Angelo.

His first temptation (Act II, Scene ii) is extremely subtle. On Isabella's part it is unconscious. Her obvious purity awakens his latent sensuality; but we do not realise that this is happening until she reaches the line:

> Go to your bosom;
> Knock there, and ask your heart what it doth know
> That's like my brother's fault; if it confess
> A natural guiltiness such as is his,
> Let it not sound a thought upon your tongue
> Against my brother's life.

And Angelo murmurs, aside:

> She speaks, and 'tis
> Such sense, that my sense breeds with it.

Now we know that he is being tempted. Earlier, when she had beautifully presented the ideal of mercy, he had been unmoved:

> It is the law, not I condemn your brother.
> ... he must die to-morrow.

Now, he prevaricates:

> Well, come to me to-morrow.

And as soon as she has gone, he is in a chaos of conflict, displayed, as usual, in a long soliloquy:

> What's this? what's this? Is this her fault or mine?
> The tempter or the tempted, who sins most? ...
> O, cunning enemy, that, to catch a saint,
> With saints dost bait thy hook! Most dangerous
> Is that temptation that doth goad us on
> To sin in loving virtue.

His second temptation and conflict (Act II, Scene iv), when she comes back to him, are inextricably interwoven. Her mere presence is temptation, increased by every look he gives her. And he is already in conflict when she enters, and so remains:

> When I would pray and think, I think and pray
> To several subjects. Heaven hath my empty words;
> Whilst my invention, hearing not my tongue,
> Anchors on Isabel ...
>   ... O, heavens!
> Why does my blood thus master to my heart?

Then comes his fall; and he makes her the following offer:

>   ... redeem thy brother
> By yielding up thy body to my will;
> Or else he must not only die the death,
> But thy unkindness shall his death draw out
> To lingering sufferance.

Isabella refuses. And she does so in words that show up her own deficiency; but we will isolate her thread presently. Keeping to Angelo, we have now reached the point in the pattern where we should expect the tragic act.

But here Shakespeare complicates the plot in two ways; for it is his intention to show that Angelo is morally guilty, and yet to avoid a tragic climax. The duke, therefore, although still in disguise, begins to pull the strings.

Angelo, we now learn, once had a sweetheart, Mariana. Although he jilted her unkindly, for reasons of pride, she loves him still; and the duke so arranges it that she shall come to him in the night, disguised as Isabella. So Angelo, in the darkness, makes love to his true sweetheart, but supposes her to be his paramour. He ought now, according to his agreement, to reprieve Claudio. But – and this is the real act of darkness – he does not. Shakespeare picks up again a theme from *Hamlet*: the unending sequence of revenge. Angelo dare not pardon Claudio; because Claudio would, if he lived and knew the truth, seek revenge. Once again, still in secret, the duke intervenes. Angelo believes the execution of Claudio to have taken place; but, in fact, it has not. Morally, however, Angelo has committed the tragic act; he believes in his own guilt; and he experiences the realisation of horror:

> This deed unshapes me quite ...
>   ... he should have lived
> Save that his riotous youth, with dangerous sense,
> Might in the times to come have ta'en revenge ...
>   ... would yet he had lived!
> Alack, when once our grace we have forgot,
> Nothing goes right: we would, and we would not.

Angelo has now exhibited the whole of Shakespeare's tragic pattern symbolically; and when he is finally unmasked by the duke, in the fifth act, he knows himself that his end should be death:

61

> Then, good prince,
> No longer session hold upon my shame,
> But let my trial be mine own confession;
> Immediate sentence then, and sequent death,
> Is all the grace I beg.

Instead of death, Angelo gets not merely mercy and a loving bride, but, we are meant to infer, re-education as well. By what means the duke is able to bring this about we must shortly enquire. But first we will follow the thread of Angelo's feminine counterpart, Isabella.

'Who sins most,' Angelo has asked, 'the tempter or the tempted?'

Allegorically speaking, Shakespeare answers this by making the tempter an objectified quality of the soul of the tempted. If it were not so, the tempted would not fall. The allegorical construction of Angelo's temptations is admirable. In the first, the saint-like Isabella, supported by the libertine Lucio, tempts the seeming saint and the unconscious libertine in Angelo. In the second temptation Lucio is unnecessary; because the quality he stands for is fully realised in Angelo himself. And the saint-like Isabella quickly turns into a demon; thus objectifying the transformtion in Angelo, for whom 'good angel' is now but a label on 'the devil's horn'.

But, besides this, Isabella is a person in her own right. Shakespeare has given her some of the most beautiful lines he ever wrote, and also, from the point of view of the character of the speaker, some of the vilest. When she speaks of mercy, and its relation to justice and temporal power, she can rise to sublimity; but she is equally capable of behaving 'like an angry ape'.

Shakespeare makes her the voice of one of his own guiding principles in the line:

And He that might the vantage best have took
Found out the remedy.

To find out the remedy – but not by re-stating theological dogma – is what this, and some of the later plays, set out to do. Shakespeare could hardly have paid Isabella a greater compliment. But the remedy that instantly suggests itself to her, as compensation for her own wrongs, is a horrid echo of the unregenerate ages:

O, I will to him and pluck out his eyes!
Injurious world! most damned Angelo!

Shakespeare is not mainly concerned, here, with characterisation in the sense that modern dramatists understand it. Isabella is self-contradictory because she is being put in the dock equally with Angelo, whom she is condemning, in just the same way as Angelo is already in the dock beside Claudio, whom he has sentenced. They both exemplify the line:

Thieves for their robbery have authority
When judges steal ...

Isabella would certainly have executed a bloody revenge on Angelo had she been able. She also, but for the duke, would have followed the tragic formula to a deed of darkness. And we may notice how faithful Shakespeare is to his own principles of construction in putting her through the preliminary temptations.

It is obviously understandable that Isabella would have been reluctant to have saved her brother from death – even though it was to be death by slow torture – by the sacrifice of her chastity. Are we, then, entitled to call her refusal to do so a yielding to temptation? When Angelo says to her:

> Be what you are,
> That is, a woman; if you be more, you're none ...

it seems like a strange presage of Macbeth:

> I dare do all that may become a man
> Who dares do more is none.

Are both of them, perhaps, guilty of hubris – the pride of attempting to overstep, in the wrong way, the measure of humanity?

With regard to Isabella, the answer seems to be yes. Her painful situation is one in which it would have been easy for Shakespeare to have retained our sympathy for her. But he alienates it, deliberately. In her reaction to Angelo's proposal he is exemplifying to us 'the goodness that is cheap in beauty'. Whether she ought to have made the particular sacrifice or not (and we might contrast her with Sonia, in Dostoevsky's *Crime and Punishment*), her manner of refusing to do so places her in the dock. From Shakespeare's point of view, she has been exposed to a subtle temptation – not simply as it appears on the surface of the scene – and she has fallen. She signally fails his standard of humanity, when she says of her brother:

> ... had he twenty heads to tender down
> On twenty bloody blocks, he'd yield them up,

64

Before his sister should her body stoop
To such abhorr'd pollution.
Then, Isabel, live chaste, and, brother, die:
More than our brother is our chastity.

Shakespeare is not making fun of chastity – far from it;
but he has purposely taken away our sympathy from
Isabella, and he continues to do so in her next scene.
Why?

If Shakespeare in *Measure for Measure*, and in some later
plays, shows himself to be an optimist, he is, one might
say, a spiritual optimist. There is no facile optimism in his
work at all. The happy ending (except where there is a
duke to intervene) depends on making the right answer to
the tragic temptation, which, if yielded to, leads on to the
act of darkness. Shakespeare is fully aware how difficult
it is, even in the more obvious cases, to make the right
answer. Sometimes it is impossible; but the first step
towards doing so is to recognise the tempter's voice. This
is not always easy: the devil can quote scripture and
assume a pleasing shape. And Shakespeare has many
characters – of which Angelo and Isabella are examples –
who are tempted and fall by what they believe to be their
virtues.

It need scarcely be said that Shakespeare does not
approve of loose living; lust has never been characterised
better than in the phrase from the sonnets, 'The expense
of spirit in a waste of shame.' Nevertheless, the exalting of
chastity above life and humanity is, in his view, a moral
fault. This is Isabella's temptation, to which she yields;
and it would have led on, as we have seen, to the full tragic
climax – her brother's death by torture, and the plucking
out of Angelo's eyes.

It is partly to help the audience to see this difficult point that Shakespeare makes Isabella so unsympathetic, although she is redeemed at the end of the play. In her second temptation – the scene where she visits her condemned brother in prison – he gives her a speech which makes her morally repulsive and shows her once more as an example of goodness cheap in beauty. We are led up to this appalling outburst by the revival of two significant themes. When Claudio, at the beginning of their interview, seems to agree with her standard, she exclaims:

> ... there my father's grave
> Did utter forth a voice.

We are back with Hamlet's ghost. When he ceases to agree, she begins to doubt her mother's marital fidelity, and we recall Laertes:

> That drop of blood that's calm proclaims me bastard!

Claudio makes her his appeal:

> Sweet sister, let me live:
> What sin you do to save a brother's life,
> Nature dispenses with the deed so far
> That it becomes a virtue.

Her reply to this, coming from a sister to a brother who is about to be tortured to death, is one of the most venomous speeches that Shakespeare ever penned:

> O, you beast!
> O faithless coward! O dishonest wretch! ...
> Take my defiance!
> Die, perish! Might but my bending down
> Reprieve thee from thy fate, it should proceed.

I'll pray a thousand prayers for thy death,
No word to save thee. ...
Mercy to thee would prove itself a bawd:
'Tis best thou diest quickly.

Shakespeare could hardly have contrived for her a more conspicuous fall, when we remember how well, how beautifully, how truly she spoke of mercy in the previous act:

Not the king's crown, nor the deputed sword,
The marshal's truncheon, nor the judge's robe,
Becomes them with one half so good a grace
As mercy does ...
I would to heaven I had your potency,
And you were Isabel! should it then be thus?
No!

But, Yes! She has ranged herself with Angelo, or rather Shakespeare has done so. She could not, now, have averted a tragic end: only with the duke's assistance does she find the light, and lose her virginity, at last.

7

Measure for Measure:
Creative Mercy

SHAKESPEARE'S purpose is now beginning to stand out clearly. He has two characters – Angelo and Isabella – whom he has put through his tragic sequence up to a point at which the natural outcome would be the same as in *Hamlet* – a stage littered with corpses. But in *Measure for Measure* he is showing us the resolution of *Hamlet*. He is telling us that tragedy, even on the threshold of its consummation, is not inevitable. And he is examining the conditions – or, more exactly, one possible set of conditions – by which it can be averted. What are they? The intervention of the duke. But what is the significance of the duke? It is something more than his character in the ordinary sense. The clue is given to us in the fifth act: he has made himself a channel for 'power divine'. Shakespeare's proposition is this: events move to a natural, that is a logically foreseeable, conclusion; but there is something higher than nature and logic. Spiritual power is always paramount; and when it is invoked, in the right way, it can arrest the tragic course.

We may now try to answer a question that confronted us before: if strict legalism would make the world a cemetery, and *laissez-faire* would reduce it to chaos, in what way does creative mercy, where these have failed, succeed? Shakespeare's reply to this is his creation of the Duke of Vienna, who exemplifies the action of creative mercy. How he does so is what we must further consider.

Shakespeare's philosophy, although expanding from play to play, is consistent throughout. The background of the duke (as of Prospero, in *The Tempest*) is that he does what Polonius told Laertes to do – he is true, first of all, to his own self. Escalus, who of all characters in the play probably knew the duke best, so describes him:

> One that, above all other strifes, contended especially to know himself.

Like Prospero, he has cultivated self-knowledge and loved 'the life removed'; but, unlike Prospero, he has not neglected his ducal responsibilities. He says to Angelo:

> Thyself and thy belongings
> Are not thine own so proper, as to waste
> Thyself upon thy virtues, they on thee.

His studies and meditations, so far from being detrimental to his duties of rulership, are conducive to their perfect discharge. It is necessary to know oneself, to cultivate virtue and the life removed; these are the foundations, and yet they are not the superstructure of perfection. The duke had 'power divine'; and the next pointer to its attainment is in the lines:

> Heaven doth with us as we with torches do,
> Not light them for themselves; for if our virtues
> Did not go forth of us, 'twere all alike
> As if we had them not.

This introduces two new themes. The first is only hinted at – that we should shape ourselves upon a pattern that is laid up in heaven; it is not elaborated here, but it is not forgotten; and it is revived in the final plays as 'integrity to heaven'. The second is the dominant theme of *Measure for Measure*: the contrast between seeming virtue and forth-going virtue. Seeming virtue is little more than vanity and self-ornament; forth-going virtue is the secret of the duke's power. But what is it, apart from the necessary background of self-knowledge, that makes virtue forth-going? The duke speaks of 'the love I have in doing good'. And when we consider the significance of the closing scene (and the argument of other plays), we shall find that the power that makes virtue go forth is love. Briefly, the duke's success in averting the tragic end depends on three indispensable conditions: knowledge of and fidelity to his own self, forth-going virtue, and love. Possessing these, he may bear 'the sword of heaven', and make creative mercy a regenerative power.

It is precisely with regard to these three qualities that the duke is contrasted with Angelo and Isabella. These seemers lack self-knowledge; but their chief deficiency is that they are unloving; therefore, they are only arrayed in virtue – it cannot shine forth as spiritual power. Nevertheless, the virtues that are only self-ornament deceive everyone in the play, their possessors included, except the duke. Escalus says of Angelo:

> If any in Vienna be of worth
> To undergo such ample grace and honour,
> It is Lord Angelo.

And Lucio says to Isabella:

> I hold you as a thing ensky'd and sainted;
> By your renouncement, an immortal spirit ...

The apparent good qualities in Angelo and Isabella are not, of course, specious in themselves; it is only that they have no real foundation. That is what the duke is planning to give them – self-knowledge and love. When he does so, in the last act, the seeming virtues will become real. In this way, creative mercy is finally revealed as a regenerative principle.

Angelo and Isabella are hard cases, and their re-education is not perfect until the end. The duke begins his psychotherapy with two patients whose moral sickness is less severe – the pair of wayward lovers, Claudio and Juliet. The lovers are in prison; Claudio under sentence of death, and Juliet awaiting the birth of her illegitimate child. The duke, who is disguised as a monk, visits the prison in this religious capacity.

Shakespeare sets Juliet in conspicuous contrast to Isabella. Juliet has seeming sin and real love: Isabella has seeming virtue and no love. The duke's treatment of each is appropriately contrasted also. With Juliet, he builds upon her love to create virtue; with Isabella, he instils love to make her virtues true. The moral healing of Juliet is far easier, and is outlined for us with beautiful concinnity. The scene is prison. The speakers are the duke, in the guise of a monk, and Juliet, as a sad expectant mother. He asks her if she repents her fault, and she answers that she does. He then says:

Love you the man that wrong'd you?

And she replies:

Yes; as I love the woman that wronged him.

From the duke's point of view, this, so far as it goes, is the right answer; for we see, when his plan unfolds in the last act, that he is making the assumption that a seed of true human love in the heart will blossom as divine love in the soul. The idea has some resemblance to Plato's belief in the gradually expanding recognition of the beautiful, and it is the perfect love that the duke is hoping to foster. He therefore points out to Juliet that if she repents only because of the public shame her lapse has brought upon her, then it is an imperfect repentance – not springing from love of heaven, but from fear of punishment:

> Which sorrow is always towards ourselves, not heaven,
> Showing we would not spare heaven as we love it,
> But as we stand in fear ...

Juliet breaks in:

> I do repent me, as it is an evil,
> And take the shame with joy.

This is the perfect answer. The duke's theory of government is that his subjects should be brought to do right not from fear of the law but from love of heaven – meaning, of course, a state of divine harmony in their own souls. Juliet, his simplest case, is thus brought to a successful conclusion, and he says:

> There rest.

The next patient is Claudio, and the task is somewhat harder. Claudio is a more divided character than Juliet; he is under sentence of death, and although he faces this well to begin with, in his heart he is afraid to die. The duke's first aim is to remove this fear. And he reasons along these lines. There is a kind of life – the life of the body which you have been condemned to lose – that is really no more than 'death's fool'; for it is always running away from death, yet always travelling deathwards: and there is also a kind of self, that is 'not thyself'; for it is compounded merely of 'many a thousand grains that issue out of dust'. This kind of life and this kind of self are things 'that none but fools would keep'. And at the end of the duke's long speech, Claudio seems convinced, for he answers:

> I humbly thank you.
> To sue to live, I find I seek to die;
> And, seeking death, find life: let it come on.

In what way Claudio has, or thinks he has, found life through death is not made explicit here. But the duke's thought is clearly moving along well-known lines of negative meditation – exposing seeming life and seeming self as a preliminary to discovering the higher realities of each. We are to assume, from Claudio's reply, that he has caught the drift of the argument; and for the benefit of the audience, the point has already been made, in a speech by Isabella in the previous act, where man was said to be –

> Most ignorant of what he's most assured,
> His glassy essence ...

The duke's discourse aimed to persuade Claudio that the life he has been doomed to lose is at best precarious, and to imply that he may, on the other hand, be assured of his 'glassy essence', that is, his spiritual nature. The argument, old as religion itself, is not original. But it establishes one point regarding Shakespeare's own philosophy which illumines other plays.

> Thou art not thyself;
> For thou exist'st on many a thousand grains
> That issue out of dust.

In play after play, Shakespeare stresses, positively, the necessity of self-knowledge, if the crucial temptation scenes are to be turned away from tragedy and towards the enhancement of life. And he is touching the same theme here, but negatively: the dust grains are not *thyself*. And so the reiterated admonition, 'to thine own self be true', means transcending one's earthy nature and being true to the spiritual being that man really is.

This is in complete conformity with the general proposition of *Measure for Measure* which we have already noticed – that the intervention of spiritual power, even on the brink of the last calamity, can arrest the tragic course. Therefore, in the final act, the duke exhibits 'power divine'; and if he had not been able to do so, the end of the play would have been death.

When the duke leaves him, Claudio's fear of death gradually returns; and he makes his touching but fruitless appeal to Isabella:

> Sweet sister, let me live.

This, and Isabella's reply, is overheard by the duke. He comes back, helps Claudio to recover his peace of mind, and leaves him with almost the same words with which he parted from Juliet:

> Hold you there: farewell.

To Isabella, he makes some cryptic remarks, the point of which she probably missed. He tells her that 'the goodness that is cheap in beauty makes beauty brief in goodness'. This is her state at the moment; but he foretells her redemption by grace – which we witness later. The plan is then made for Mariana to visit Angelo in disguise.

Much might be said of the under-plot; but for the sake of clarity we shall only follow the main characters here; and so we will pass directly to the re-education, or redemption, of Angelo and Isabella in the last act. The duke, his disguise laid aside, returns to Vienna to resume authority. Angelo is seemingly virtuous still; but morally he has committed fornication and murder, and believes himself to be guilty of both. The sainted Isabella, more self-righteous than ever, is clamouring for a bloody revenge: justice is what she demands, and no more fine speeches about mercy. When it seems that she may not get it, she exclaims:

> O, you blessed ministers above,
> Keep me in patience, and with ripen'd time
> Unfold the evil which is here wrapt up …

Every tragic ending is an answer to this prayer. But for the duke, it would have been answered – and whipping or beheading been the portion of them all.

Angelo, on whom the duke is now cunningly at work, is first allowed – or lured – to judge his own case; for to make a rigorous application of one's own precepts to one's own practices is conducive both to knowledge of oneself and mercy towards others – two lessons which the duke is determined to teach. And Angelo is intended to feel the prick of the duke's observation to Lucio:

> … when you have
> A business for yourself, pray heaven you then
> Be perfect.

When Angelo is at length unmasked, he does – to do him

75

credit – in effect pass sentence on himself in conformity with his own code:

> ... I crave death more willingly than mercy;
> 'Tis my deserving, and I do entreat it.

And the duke, as it seems, has already confirmed this:

> An Angelo for a Claudio, death for death.

Claudio, of course, is only thought to be dead, and will shortly reappear; and the duke has no intention of hanging anyone; but for passing the death sentence, or confirming it, he has several reasons. The most general of these is to illustrate the principle that Shakespeare never tires of reiterating: that unless there be forgiveness and love there is no hope for any of us. 'Death for death' – it might have been the title of *Hamlet*. A further reason is that this is a part of what I have called the duke's shock-therapy: to be prepared for death, in the proper way, is to gain a fuller realisation of life:

> That life is better life, past fearing death,
> Than that which lives to fear ...

From the outset, therefore, it was the duke's intention to let the logically tragic climax almost come – so as to give his erring subjects an awakening shock. Having faced death, they will have learnt to live better:

> Be absolute for death; either death or life
> Shall thereby be the sweeter.

Shakespeare has been accused, in this last act, of pandering to a love of theatrical effect; he certainly uses theatrical effect, but he never pandered to it less; he is proceeding with an ethical demonstration:

76

By cold gradation and well-balanced form.

He never compromises his argument; but some sacrifices are made to it of realistic characterisation.

Claudio has been faced with death; Angelo is faced with death; Juliet, Mariana and Isabella have been faced with a lover's or a brother's death: and each of them is to be the recipient of more abundant life. From first to last, all is plan. After the duke's discourse to him in prison, Claudio could rise to the thought:

> If I must die,
> I will encounter darkness as a bride,
> And hug it in mine arms.

And the duke's line of treatment is implicit there; for he prepares his patients for darkness, but he gives them each a bride.

The last drop of the curtain in *Hamlet* is on a pile of corpses: in *Measure for Measure*, on a series of unions of love. The contrast is as vivid as Shakespeare can make it – grief of death to the topmost joy of life. And the implication is that the prerequisites of that grace which keeps the body ever fair are forgiveness and love. This is the final reason why Angelo must be sentenced to die. Isabella has yet to be redeemed; but there is no redemption without forgiveness. Shakespeare has placed her morally in the dock beside Angelo; and now, though she does not suspect it, she is on trial with him. Angelo is her enemy. If she forgives him and intercedes for him, she will be saved; and the duke will offer her his love. If she does not – we can only suppose that she would have gone back to her convent, to a life of bitterness and seeming virtue, perpetually immured.

What saves her from this fate? Not her own self-adorning 'goodness', but a living example of love. Mariana, who is true to Angelo in spite of everything, implores her:

> Isabel,
> Sweet Isabel, do yet but kneel by me;
> Hold up your hands, say nothing, I'll speak all.
> They say, best men are moulded out of faults;
> And, for the most, become much more the better
> For being a little bad: so may my husband.
> O Isabel, will you not lend a knee?

She does, and she has her reward from the duke:

> ... for your lovely sake,
> Give me your hand, and say you will be mine ...

On Mariana, the duke bestows his benediction; and to Angelo he displays the power of creative mercy, which it was the purpose of the play to reveal:

> Joy to you, Mariana! Love her, Angelo.

We are left to suppose that Angelo does; and that, because he does, his lifeless virtues become forth-going powers.

So many trivial comedies end with wedding-bells that this may seem commonplace. But Shakespeare has not reached his happy ending by facile emotion; he has followed his principles of dramatic construction, which parallel his ethical beliefs, and he has arrived at love by the path of reason. *Hamlet* left him with a problem in ethics: in *Measure for Measure* he solves it, phase by phase, with a lucid *intelletto d'amore*.*

---

* '... ladies that have intelligence of love', *Purgatorio* XXIV.

There is also in *Measure for Measure* a beautifully propor-
tioned allegorical structure. And the allegorical figures
that group round Angelo are very like those around
Hamlet. Ophelia is represented by Mariana. Both of them
represent the soul's guiding star of love; both of them are
rejected for the same reason, because the ways of life that
Hamlet and Angelo have chosen lead deathwards and are
incompatible with the way of love; both pray, in effect,
'O, help him, you sweet Heavens!' Ophelia is lost in
Hamlet's self-destruction; Mariana becomes Angelo's
unfolding star.

Polonius reappears in Escalus: both are fidelity. In the
case of Escalus, it is fidelity to the merciful standards of
the absent duke, which are equally the standards of the
positive aspect of 'thine own self'. Angelo does not kill
'the good old man'; but he has no patience with him, and
refuses, during the tragic part of his course, to follow his
advice. When Mariana is relegated to her moated grange
and Escalus is unheeded, it is to say, allegorically, that
Angelo, like Hamlet, has expelled love and fidelity from
his own soul. The outcome for each of them is identical.
Their souls do not remain empty; when the good qualities
have been thrust out, a demon steps in; for if Isabella
could have had her way with Angelo, unguided by the
duke, she would have brought vengeance upon him –
'death for death' – as assuredly as Laertes did on Hamlet.

Hamlet and Angelo both stand well in the world's
opinion. Both doom a man to die. Their sentences – on
Claudius and Claudio respectively – are justifiable according to the letter of the old law, but not according to the
spirit of the new. The predicaments of these judges run
parallel. But there is one vast difference between them.

With Hamlet is the ghost, dragging him back; with Angelo is the duke, helping him on. If these plays were staged on successive nights, with the same cast, they would illuminate each other.

Measure for Measure has sometimes been interpreted as a sermon on the text that 'power corrupts'; but Shakespeare never says this. The real power is always retained by the duke, and in his hands it is life-giving. It is certainly a corollary of the play's main theme that power reveals: authority will display a corruption that is already there, but it will equally give scope to the love of doing good. If the seemers are exposed by it, so, also, are the true. Shakespeare was never an anarchist; and when he studies the problem of power, he does not suggest that it can be solved by abolition. His solution is an aristocracy of the spirit; his qualifications for rulership are self-realisation, forgiveness and love; and his ideal is a philosopher, or perhaps a mystic king.

I have omitted the under-plot, in order to stress the dominant themes; but its existence must not be forgotten. It illustrates the principle of equipoise in construction, which is so remarkable a feature of Shakespeare's mind. The unbalance of Angelo and Isabella in one direction is set against that of Pompey and Mistress Overdone in the other; and both are rectified by the duke's ideal of self-knowledge and love. Psychologically, the Eros element in the play is handled in a manner that seems amazingly modern, and might have been guided by a quotation from Jung:

> Eros is a questionable fellow and will always remain so, whatever the legislation of the future may have to say about it. He belongs on one side to man's primordial animal nature

which will endure as long as man has an animal body. On the other side, he is related to the highest forms of the spirit. But he only thrives when spirit and instinct are in right harmony. If one or the other is lacking to him, the result is injury or at least a lopsidedness that may easily veer towards the pathological.*

Students of Jung's psychology will, I think, hand it to Shakespeare that *Measure for Measure* illustrates this theme to perfection; for it not only makes a similar diagnosis, both as regards the individual and society, but it also sets out the treatment; one outcome of the unions of love is to bring spirit and instinct into harmony. But in saying that Shakespeare deals with this problem in a manner that shows correspondences with psychiatry, I do not mean that he had a modern attitude of mind. In some respects it would no doubt be true to say that he was ahead of his time; but if by this we imply the compliment that he was rather more like us than his fellow Elizabethans, then we cannot be sure that he would have felt flattered, and I doubt very much if it is so. It is rather that he was beyond his time, in the sense that he saw more deeply into life than all but a few men have done in any age; this does not necessarily make his views resemble ours, and might even have the opposite effect: it certainly brings him nearer to Plato than to Marx. His debt to the Middle Ages is very great, and it includes their respect for logic. This is fortunate for us; because it means that he develops his ideas, though often veiled in allegory, with a consistency that we discover we can trust.

* Jung, *Two Essays on Analytical Psychology*, Collected Works, Vol. VII, p.27.

8

The Plays as Allegory

BEFORE WE LEAVE *Measure for Measure*, there is one speculation about it that must be mentioned. Was it intended as an allegory of government by the Church in the seeming absence of Christ?

In the strict sense, it does not appear so; and yet there are compelling reasons for thinking that the idea was in Shakespeare's mind – and he possessed a bewildering ability of doing several things at once. If he so intended it, we may notice that he wrote a criticism, but not a satire. Critical reflections on the discrepancy between the practices of the Church and the precepts of the Gospels were widespread in his time. Thoughts so awakened, in some form, were a visitation he could not have avoided.

Shakespeare was well aware, to take a single example, that Sir Walter Raleigh's circle of friends and clients was dangerously outspoken on such matters, and that Marlowe, a member of the circle, had been accused of 'atheism'. The charge against Marlowe was absurd, by philosophical standards; but the Reformation had not, of itself, made unorthodoxy safe. The legal enquiry into Raleigh's own opinions, although it came to nothing, was for a while a *cause célèbre*. These were problems of the

period which all thoughtful men were compelled to pon-
der, and Raleigh expressed his own opinion bluntly:

> Say to the Church it shows
> What's good, and doth no good.

Shakespeare was not of Raleigh's faction, but a man of
his moral insight, especially in an age when Christendom
was riven by religious war, could not have considered the
conduct of the Churches to be Christlike. The trend of
his own philosophy, as revealed in successive plays, was
towards a syncretism of Classical reason and Christian
grace: from the oracle of Apollo comes the whisper of
redemption; and he lays emphasis increasingly on the
ethics of the New Testament and repudiates those of
the Old. It is on this last point – even if he had had no
predecessors of the same opinion – that Shakespeare
would have been critical of the Churches. He believed in
the higher morality of the Gospels; and they, apparently,
did not.

It is unlikely that he would have kept silence on this
subject. But he had such an amazing gift of allegorical
presentation that he could have said far more than
Marlowe without falling foul of the law. Even apart from
the dangers of prosecution, he preferred to express his
deepest thoughts most subtly. He probably wrote for two
publics: dramatically for the many, and philosophically for
the few.

> ... we have with special soul
> Elected him our absence to supply;
> Lent him our terror, dress'd him with our love,
> And given his deputation all the organs
> Of our own power.

The duke is referring to Angelo; and in the next scene, he adds:

> And to behold his sway
> I will, as 'twere a brother of your order,
> Visit both prince and people.

The passages may mean no more than they appear to say; but if Shakespeare had been intending to convey that the regency of the Church was under divine observation, he would have been likely to do so in just such a way. And as the duke, in his humble disguise, moves through the play, there are moments when the aura of a religious figure gathers round him. 'Of whence are you?' Escalus asks him as they stand before the prison, and the duke replies:

> Not of this country, though my chance is now
> To use it for my time: I am a brother
> Of gracious order, late come from the See
> In special business from his Holiness.

In the England of Shakespeare's day, such reverence was not shown to Rome; and when Shakespeare writes passages of this kind, they are purposeful. The least we can infer is that the duke was specially conscious of performing the will of heaven; and if he was not intended to be a symbol of Christ, he was certainly engaged upon a Christ-like task. The lengthy prose speech* which follows is a challenge to interpretation; and to attribute to it a religious significance is surely not, in the context, to force the meaning.

In this speech the duke makes some cryptic affirmations: goodness is so sick that it must die in order to be

---

* See Wilson Knight, *The Wheel of Fire*.

cured, there is a course that it is dangerous to continue in, there is a kind of security that makes human fellowships accursed; and in contradistinction to these, there is a newness that is asked for but not accepted, an undertaking in which it is virtuous to be constant, and truth of which there is too little. The general sense is not in doubt: something old must go, and something new must come. And in view of the religious build-up that the duke has just been given, and of the philosophic matrix of the play contrasted with that of *Hamlet*, Shakespeare almost certainly meant that the ethics of the Old Testament must be repudiated before it is possible to live by those of the New.

The inference that would, then, be intended, is that the Churches do not do this. They do not rely on the higher morality of the Gospels; they do not believe in the practicability of turning the other cheek, of refraining from judgment, of overcoming evil by good alone, and of being perfect: like Angelo, they judge, imprison, excommunicate and reluctantly approve of hanging.

Shakespeare does not support a compromise between the old and the new. In opposing *Measure for Measure* to *Hamlet*, he presents a choice. And if Angelo and the Church were linked in his mind, he is saying that if the Church would give up the harsh judgments of the Old Testament, and trust in the creative mercy of the New, it would realise its spiritual power. For although the duke possesses temporal power, what is stressed as the play comes to its climax is the spiritual power that gathers round him; and this is not a fortuitous endowment, but a product of his way of life. There comes a moment, in the last act, when Angelo knows that the duke can see into his soul; and then he no longer tries to brazen out his conduct, but falls upon his knees:

> O, my dread lord,
> I should be guiltier than my guiltiness,
> To think I can be undiscernible,
> When I perceive your Grace, like power divine,
> Hath look'd upon my passes.

Did Shakespeare mean this to be the Church revisited by Christ? The play is not a sustained allegory to that effect; and yet it seems inescapable that the idea was in his mind, and that here, and in some other scenes and speeches, it took partial shape. If so, his criticism is creative and his conclusion of good hope. Angelo repents, his false virtue is made true, he is set right and forgiven. So, too, are all those he had condemned. The only judgment done on them is that they are turned from the tragic course of Macbeth – leading to 'O, horror! horror! horror!' – to the way of regeneration and light.

9

Othello: How Tragedy Progresses

WHEN THE KING prays, in *Hamlet*, referring to his bloodstained hand, he says:

Is there not rain enough in the sweet heavens
To wash it white as snow? Whereto serves mercy
But to confront the visage of offence?

In *Measure for Measure*, Shakespeare answered these queries. When creative mercy confronts the visage of offence, it does call down the lustral rain from heaven. This is one resolution of tragedy, but not the only one. Towards the end of his prayer, the sinning king himself has intimations of another way:

What then? what rests?
Try what repentance can: what can it not?

These might be merely rhetorical questions; or they might receive a ready-made answer from the dusty tomes of the seminary; but they would seem to have re-echoed in Shakespeare's mind, until he found a reply that satisfied himself. He imparts it to us in another pair of plays – a tragedy and its resolution – *Othello* and *The Winter's Tale*.

In *Othello*, Shakespeare is making a special study of the nature and process of temptation. That is why the tempter's voice – Iago – is so developed a 'character'. He is in the first scene, and in the last: the action lies enfolded in his mind. In this, he is like the Duke of Vienna; and he is like him also in that both move through their respective plays pulling the wires, controlling the plots – the one for evil and the other for good. It is probable that *Measure for Measure* and *Othello* were written in the same year, 1604, and that *Hamlet* immediately preceded them. Hamlet, Angelo, Othello – the ghost, the duke, Iago: with each protagonist is his *éminence grise*.*

Allegorically, the relationship is closer. The directing figure, embodied for dramatic presentation, is not only with but also within the hero. Shakespeare's picture of the soul is a kingdom in which rival powers are contending; this kingdom within, when the true self is enthroned, will become 'the kingdom of heaven'; but, in man's tragic phase, it is a kingdom in civil war.

In Shakespeare's plays, everything happens first in the soul; and what he shows us on the stage – and the world was a stage in his view – is the embodiment of these psychic events. This explains his curious emphasis, in many places, that seeming something comes from seeming nothing. The soul, a seeming nothing, creates; and the world, a seeming something, embodies.

Only allegory can present such conceptions in the theatre; and if we miss the allegory in Shakespeare, we miss his mind; we still have, it is true, the magnificent raiment of his thoughts; but not the life they spring from. Even to glimpse this, we must continually insist on the dual nature of certain characters, that they are both

* Confidential agent, especially one who exercises power unofficially (applied originally to Cardinal Richelieu's private secretary – literally "grey cardinal").

real and allegorical at the same time, and that their full significance includes both these aspects. It is difficult for us to appreciate this principle of construction, because our outlook is so different from Shakespeare's. Our background is the rationalism of the eighteenth and nineteenth centuries, while his was the mysticism of the Middle Ages; we look at him across the age of reason, and are apt to forget that he knew nothing of it; since the *éclaircissement*,* Europe has been sharpening its intellect, but in an earlier age it was much more interested in the exploration of its soul. The men of the renaissance stand between. And every blossoming of civilisation is partly promise of the future, but mainly a summation of the past.

Whenever a Shakespearean hero has behind him an *éminence grise* – pulling the strings so effectually that the hero sometimes seems to be his puppet – the background character embodies some content of the hero's soul; and since his soul, in the tragedies, is in conflict, the controlling personage represents that aspect which, for the purpose of the particular play, is, or will be, dominant. The soul's battle is not finally lost or won in a single play, but continues until the true self wins: before that happens, there are many ebbs and flows in the conflict, and many usurpations. We may say that the duke is symbolic of Angelo's true self, and the outcome of the play is a spiritual victory: the ghost and Iago, on the other hand, represent usurping powers, temporarily dominating the souls of Hamlet and Othello, and the consequence is a spiritual defeat. But for Shakespeare these tragic defeats are not ultimate. A battle was lost in *Hamlet*, but in *Measure for*

* A revelation, resolution of a misunderstanding between two parties, or clarification.

Measure a war was won. It is the same in the pair of plays we are about to consider.

We have seen that the first two phases of Shakespearean tragedy characterise the tempter and exhibit the flaw in the hero's soul. Sometimes Shakespeare integrates these closely: Iago is jealousy, and jealousy is the flaw in Othello's soul. In the opening dialogue we find that Iago is jealous of Cassio, and it is against Cassio that Othello's jealousy is later turned.

Iago ends his third speech with words that are Shakespeare's hall-mark of base or imperfect metal:

> I am not what I am.

Since we know Shakespeare's standard of integrity – 'I am that I am' – we can be quite certain that we are dealing with a villain. It has already been intimated that jealousy is the spur to his villainy, and Othello the victim. And because, according to Shakespeare's scheme, a soul is never the victim of anything but its own defects, we may guess that jealousy will be Othello's weakness. This is confirmed in the first temptation scene, when Othello exclaims to Iago:

> By Heaven, thou echoest me;
> As if there were some monster in thy thought
> Too hideous to be shown.

Where is the original sound and where the echo? In which mind is the monster and in which its reflection? 'Thou echoest me.' In such scenes, the tempter is the fault in the hero's soul made flesh.

The raising of this point, however, is to anticipate. Between Othello and Iago there is mutual stimulation at every phase. And when Iago tells us, in his soliloquy at the end of the first act, the root of his jealous hatred of Othello, the shape of the plot is prefigured:

> I hate the Moor,
> And it is thought abroad, that 'twixt my sheets
> He's done my office. I know not if't be true,
> But I, for mere suspicion in that kind,
> Will do as if for surety.

All Shakespeare's characters are sincere in their soliloquies, and Iago's jealousy is as real as Othello's: only one is cold and the other hot, one schemes and the other strikes, one is the mind and the other the deed. Both, once begun, increase. So, in the second act, Iago reveals to us that Desdemona is to be the means –

> ... to diet my revenge,
> For that I do suspect the lusty Moor
> Hath leap'd into my seat. The thought whereof
> Doth like a poisonous mineral gnaw my inwards;
> And nothing can or shall content my soul
> Till I am even'd with him, wife for wife;
> Or failing so, yet that I put the Moor
> At least into a jealousy so strong
> That judgment cannot cure.

In *Measure for Measure*, written only a few months earlier, we had the line:

> An Angelo for a Claudio, death for death.

And here we have, in effect:

> A Desdemona for an Emilia, wife for wife.

Clearly, there are variations on the same tragic theme: the unending sequence of deathdooms and revenges, until the old law is repudiated and the world learns to live by the new.

It is curious that some commentators have thought Iago to be without sufficient motive; although he expresses it more in plotting than in passion, he has as much motive as the perpetrators of most *crimes passionnels*. But had he grounds in fact? Had Othello seduced his wife? We are never directly told. Emilia, of course, denies it; but when Desdemona questions her on her opinions about fidelity in principle, saying that she would not betray her husband for the world, Emilia answers:

> The world is a huge thing; 'tis a great price
> For a small vice.
> In troth, I think I should ...

We have no evidence, nor had Iago. But there are several straws in the wind; and when we consider Leontes, in *The Winter's Tale*, the point that Shakespeare is making becomes clear: 'something' can spring from 'nothing'. Because, in Shakespeare's view, the soul is a creative power, therefore its contents, seeming nothing, may have tremendous outcomes:

> Is this nothing?
> Why, then the world and all that's in't is nothing;
> The covering sky is nothing; Bohemia nothing;
> My wife is nothing; nor nothing have these nothings,
> If this be nothing!

Leontes was mad with jealousy when he said that; but, nevertheless, beneath all those nothings is a typical Shakespearean thought: that imaginations are, in fact, bodied forth in time. And for these reasons we must suppose that Iago, Othello and Leontes all had the same grounds for their jealousy – nothing. 'Begot upon itself, born on itself'; but out of such seeming nothings, either tragedy or redemption may grow.

These two soliloquies of Iago cannot qualify as two temptations and inner conflicts; and yet they are akin to them, and have a germinal relation to the tragic pattern. They prefigure the temptations and conflicts coming to Othello. They are like poisonous seeds from which the rank plant will unfold.

We have seen that according to Shakespeare's usual, and probably earlier pattern, the inner conflict immediately follows the temptation; but it is clear that in living experience these two phases will often intermingle. In Angelo's second temptation and conflict, the last scene of the kind to be written before *Othello*, Shakespeare staged them in this way, and we watch them surging and seething together. He must have been satisfied with this effect, because both the comparable scenes in *Othello* are similarly compounded.

These scenes are, of course, Act III, Scene iii, and Act IV, Scene i. As temptation is being specially analysed in this play, they are the longest of their kind that Shakespeare wrote. It is interesting to compare them with their counterparts in *Measure for Measure*; but, for our limited purpose, they need not be further discussed here. They lead on, in the usual tragic sequence, to the deed of darkness, the realisation of horror and the hero's death.

The allegorical composition is superb. We have seen in other plays that, in Shakespeare's view, the soul is never empty: when its good qualities are thrust down to the nadir, the evil ones spring instantly to the zenith, and this is displayed to us by the hero's alternating relationships with those characters that carry an allegorical meaning. In the grave of love, the fingers of revenge closed about Hamlet's throat; because Mariana was rejected, Angelo found a revengeful demon in her place; and, in the same way, as soon as Othello disavows Desdemona, Iago is supreme. The reality of this takes place in Othello's soul. But the allegory by which it is revealed to us – the replacement of love by hate – is one of Shakespeare's supreme achievements:

> Look here, Iago;
> All my fond love thus do I blow to heaven:
> 'Tis gone.
> Arise, black vengeance, from the hollow hell!
> Yield up, O love! thy crown and hearted throne
> To tyrannous hate.

As in *Hamlet*, it is a spiritual inversion. And holy things – 'Witness, you ever-burning lights above!' and 'I greet thy love!' – are invoked for infamy. Fair is again made foul and foul fair. This dreadful conception, the rejection of the heavenly and the consequent invasion of the hellish, must have been intensely vivid in Shakespeare's mind. He allegorises it again and again; and none of the tragedies is without it. It could only have sprung from some powerful imaginative experence, possibly Marlowe's Faust. But it is my belief that Shakespeare derived the idea from the story of Judas – that when he betrayed Christ, the devil entered into him. And the life of Judas – if we imagine precedent temptations – might have been Shakespeare's paradigm of tragedy: a deed of darkness, involving the betrayal of the best, a realisation of horror, and death.

The alteration in the tragic hero, as Shakespeare allegorises it, is so extreme that we are bound to see it as an exchange of the divine for the diabolic. Ophelia prays for Hamlet:

> O heavenly powers, restore him!

And Laertes says to him:

> The devil take thy soul!

Mariana intercedes for Angelo's life:

> Lend me your knees, and all my life to come
> I'll lend you all my life to do you service.

While Isabella has said:

> O! I will to him and pluck out his eyes! ...
> Most damned Angelo!

Desdemona and Iago are contrasted in the same way. The horrific scene, in which Othello and Iago kneel together in self-dedication to evil, is closed by Othello with the lines:

> O, damn her!
> Come, go with me apart; I will withdraw
> To furnish me with some swift means of death
> For the fair devil. Thou art now my lieutenant.

And Iago answers:

> I am your own for ever.

We might well say that the devil then entered into Othello – or, more exactly, since the diabolic propensity was already there, took possession. And the names of all Shakespeare's tragic heroes are, in some essential way, 'yoked with his that did betray the Best'. But in spite of a satanic quality, they are also pathetic figures: they sell their birthright for a mess of pottage, they crucify Christ and know not what they do, and a prayer has been made in heaven for their forgiveness. In *Measure for Measure*, Shakespeare began to show how it was answered, and he continues to do so in *The Winter's Tale*.

IO

Winter's Tale:
Driving Out Good Counsel

THERE ARE SOME striking similarities of construction between *Othello* and *The Winter's Tale* which we will now consider. In both plays, the temptation begins with an innocent conversation between the hero's wife and the hero's friend. Then follows the granting of a harmless favour – in one case by wife to friend, and in the other by friend to wife. Upon that, the voice of jealousy instantly speaks:

Ha! I like not that.

In *Othello*, the tempter's voice is incarnate; in *The Winter's Tale* it is implicit. But we hear those words in Leontes' thoughts as clearly as if Iago had uttered them. Indeed, Iago might have spoken Leontes' first aside:

Too hot, too hot!
To mingle friendship far is mingling bloods.

And in a matter of minutes, in the mind of both the heroes, there is 'the green-eyed monster'.

In both of them, the inner conflict is then shown to us as an increasing fury. Othello:

> I am abused, and my relief
> Must be to loathe her. O curse of marriage!
> That we can call these delicate creatures ours,
> And not their appetites. I had rather be a toad,
> And live upon the vapour of a dungeon,
> Than keep a corner in the thing I love
> For others' uses.

And shortly after:

> If there be cords or knives,
> Poison, or fire, or suffocating streams,
> I'll not endure it.

These revealing outbursts are paralleled by those of Leontes; first, to his son, in bitter irony:

> Go, play, boy, play: thy mother plays, and I
> Play too; but so disgraced a part, whose issue
> Will hiss me to my grave.

And then, more than ever incensed by Camillo's disbelief, he begins to rage:

> Dost think I am so muddy, so unsettled,
> As to appoint myself in this vexation; sully
> The purity and whiteness of my sheets,
> Which to preserve is sleep, which being spotted
> Is goads, thorns, nettles, tails of wasps ...

In both plays also, the first temptation scene reaches the same climax: the hero's order to murder his best friend. Othello says to Iago:

> Within these three days let me hear thee say,
> That Cassio's not alive.

And Iago answers:

> My friend is dead ...

Leontes says to Camillo:

> ... and thou,
> His cupbearer ...
> ... mightst bespice a cup,
> To give mine enemy a lasting wink;
> Which draught to me were cordial. ...
> This is all:
> Do't, and thou hast the one half of my heart;
> Do't not, thou splitt'st thine own.

These scenes are clearly constructed on the same plan. And the allegory in each is the same in one respect, but in arresting contrast in another. The murder, or the will to murder Friendship, is the same; and this accords with Shakespeare's principle that the down-going soul rejects its higher qualities as it moves towards the tragic act, the consummation of which is impossible until true nobility has been overthrown. The allegorical contrast, of course, is between the counsellors. Othello being doomed, has Iago by his side, an embodiment of his revengeful jealousy; Leontes, whom Shakespeare is intending to save, has Camillo, who represents fidelity to the higher self.

Camillo belongs to the Polonius, Escalus, Gonzalo group: to follow their advice means maintaining 'integrity to heaven'. Leontes gives a hint of the allegorical relationship between himself and Camillo when, before they quarrel, he says:

> I have trusted thee, Camillo,
> With all the nearest things to my heart, as well
> My chamber-councils; wherein, priest-like, thou
> Hast cleansed my bosom, I from thee departed
> Thy penitent reformed.

Leontes is speaking of the past, and Shakespeare of the

future; for a penitent reformed is what this hero is destined to be. Meanwhile, the link between Fidelity and Friendship is affirmed by Polixenes in several speeches:

> Camillo,
> As you are certainly a gentleman, thereto
> Clerk-like experienced ...
> ... I beseech you,
> If you know aught which does behove my knowledge
> Thereof to be informed, imprison't not ...

At this, Camillo tells the truth, and Polixenes believes him:

> Give me thy hand:
> Be pilot to me and thy places shall
> Still neighbnour mine.

This is consistent with Shakespeare's constructional principles. He tends to embody those qualities of the hero's soul that will predominate. The opposing groups of qualities are always present within the hero, but not all of them are exteriorised. When the conflict is intense and prolonged, as in *Hamlet*, both groups appear. Hamlet is torn between them from the beginning. When he is about to follow the ghost, Horatio, who is friendship, holds him back:

> Be ruled; you shall not go.

At which, Hamlet draws his sword:

> Unhand me, gentlemen,
> By heaven! I'll make a ghost of him that lets me:
> I say, away! Go on, I'll follow thee.

He goes, and Horatio comments:

> He waxes desperate with imagination.

This short scene gains much in significance when compared with corresponding situations in other plays. There is, for instance, the threat to kill Friendship, which is carried much further by Othello and Leontes. There is the tearing asunder of the soul, allegorised and acted out. There is the act of decision between one group of qualities and another, and an intimation that the following of the second involves the expulsion of the first. Considered in isolation, this would be merely a dramatic incident; but as the introduction to one of Shakespeare's standard scenes of temptation it carries undertones of meaning that we cannot ignore. And, finally, Horatio's comment again expresses one of Shakespeare's most remarkable and persistent ideas: that imagination is a true creative power, from which fate itself is bodied forth.

In Leontes' second temptation (Act II, Scene i), conflict and temptation are again interwoven. The first speech he makes – he has just learnt of the flight of Camillo and Polixenes – is one of conflict:

> There may be in the cup
> A spider steep'd, and one may drink, depart,
> And yet partake no venom; for his knowledge
> Is not infected: but if one present
> The abhorr'd ingredient to his eye, make known
> How he hath drunk, he cracks his gorge, his sides,
> With violent hefts. I have drunk, and seen the spider.

It is not only the violent hefts which are important here; what is more significant is the cause of them. In reality, Leontes had drunk, and dreamed the spider; for it is a creation of his mind. But its venom is none the less potent on that account. In this play, as elsewhere, when Shakespeare

is discussing the cause and cure of tragedy, he states his
theory logically, and his major premise is implicit in
Leontes' speech: the poison is in the soul, and so is the
healing balm.

We saw that Othello and Leontes were in much the
same state at the end of their first temptations: friendship
and good counsel had been driven out; and both of them,
in effect, had said:

> Yield up, O love! thy crown and hearted throne
> To tyrannous hate.

Hate, expressed as tyranny, is now shown as their chief
characteristic; and in the second temptations it gathers
round a material object, which is at once its point of focus
and of rediffusion. For Othello it was the handkerchief; for
Leontes it is his wife's pregnancy.

Hermione had 'spread of late into a goodly bulk'; and it
is this sight (like that of Cassio with the handkerchief)
that goads Leontes most:

> ... let her sport herself
> With that she's big with; for 'tis Polixenes
> Has made thee swell thus.

And in both plays, the second temptation scenes end – as
did the first – on an identical climax: 'justice'. Iago says:

> ... strangle her in bed, even the bed she hath contaminated.

And Othello answers:

> Good, good; the justice of it pleases; very good.

Leontes says:

> Away with her to prison!

She is to await trial there, on a capital charge; for he also is seeking justice. But his courtiers expostulate:

> Be certain what you do, sir, lest your justice
> Prove violence; in the which three great ones suffer,
> Yourself, your queen, your son.

So the first temptations end with a command to murder, and the second with a demand for justice! Shakespeare's irony is devastating, and it is intended to be of wider application than to the present plots. Even the ensky'd-and-sainted one would have torn out eyes in the fourth act and still claimed justice in the last.

Shakespeare is no less preoccupied with the nature of justice than Plato was; but he pursues it with more subtlety, and makes his comments with mordant sarcasm. And he comes, as Plato did not, to an unequivocal conclusion: there is no true justice without love. Justice becomes tyranny when love yields up its crown. Angelo, Isabella, Othello and Leontes are all tyrannous in action, because they have cast out love; and when Hamlet is examined thoroughly, he is seen to be in no better case.

But Othello and Leontes are oppositely fated, and therefore there is one all-important difference at the conclusion of this scene: Leontes, in spite of his rages, has sent messengers to the oracle of Apollo. This is the crux of the play – the hero's first effort to turn from the tragic path, towards the light. Symbolically, the oracle is the higher self; therein, true rulership resides, which ought to be, and finally must be acknowledged. The answer he receives from the oracle is, in inner meaning, a message to the passions from the spirit.

The same allegory is present in *Othello*, but with a

different outcome. Directly after his second temptation, Othello receives a message from the Duke of Venice. Othello had not asked for it, but if he had obeyed it perfectly, it would have been a message of salvation; for the calm government in Venice is to the raging madness in Cyprus as cosmos to chaos. The sealed orders from the duke, and the sealed oracle of Apollo both symbolise a recall, by a higher power, to the true self. Othello did not obey this, in its deeper sense, divine summons; instead, he murdered Love – which is the irrevocable step in self-destruction.

The reaction of Leontes we will consider later; but in the meantime, Hermione, after being publicly vilified (as Desdemona was publicly vilified by Othello, Ophelia by Hamlet, and, to a much lesser degree, Mariana by Angelo), is sent to prison. And by way of neatly crossing the final *t*, Shakespeare gives her a lady-in-waiting named Emilia.

Between the second temptation and the tragic act there are two more parallel scenes. In the first of these, a woman speaks out boldly in defence of Love. Emilia says to Othello:

> I durst, my lord, to wager she is honest,
> Lay down my soul at stake: if you think other,
> Remove your thought; it doth abuse your bosom.

And Paulina, in the last of several forceful speeches, says to Leontes:

> ... this most cruel usage of your queen,
> Not able to produce more accusation
> Than your own weak-hinged fancy, something savours
> Of tyranny, and will ignoble make you,
> Yea, scandalous to the world.

The reaction of both heroes is the same – their violence

gets worse; so that in the next pair of parallel scenes we are shown a terrible outpouring of rage and hate against Love personified. This culminates, in *Othello*, with his shout:

Impudent strumpet!

A scene which Bradley thought more painful to the audience than the actual murder.

Leontes' fury is vented on Hermione's second self, her new-born daughter, the child of his own love. He says to Antigonus:

My child? away with it!
And see it instantly consumed with fire;
Even thou, and none but thou.
                        If thou refuse
And wilt encounter with my wrath, say so;
The bastard brains with these my proper hands
Shall I dash out. Go, take it to the fire ...

Antigonus, daring his wrath, pleads with him; and Leontes consents to a slightly less dreadful sentence – exposure, instead of burning:

                    We enjoin thee,
As thou art liege-man to us, that thou carry
This female bastard hence, and that thou bear it
To some remote and desert place, quite out
Of our dominions; and that there thou leave it,
Without more mercy, to its own protection ...

'Impudent strumpet!' 'Female bastard ...' And Hamlet's coarse speeches to Ophelia were to the same purpose; because the deliberate degradation of Love is one of Shakespeare's regular indications that a soul is moving towards the tragic act.

The next phase of the sequence is the deed of darkness, by the perpetration of which the hero dooms himself. In several plays, Shakespeare presents this crime, with withering irony, as a trial and an execution of justice. Brutus, Hamlet, Angelo – three 'just' men, and all of them 'honourable murderers' by act or by intention. And so it is with Othello and Leontes. There is a trial scene in *Othello*, with Othello as judge, jury, executioner – and criminal:

> It is the cause, it is the cause, my soul;
> Let me not name it to you, you chaste stars!
> It is the cause ...
> ... she must die, else she'll betray more men.
>
> O perjur'd woman! thou dost stone my heart,
> And mak'st me call what I intend to do
> A murder, which I thought a sacrifice.
> Down, strumpet!

Many other speeches are recalled by this. Brutus:

> Let us be sacrificers, but not butchers –
> Let us carve him as a dish fit for the gods.

Angelo:

> It is the law, not I condemn your brother ...
> ... he must die to-morrow.

Hamlet:

> Is't not perfect conscience
> To acquit him with this arm?

The subject is at the heart of so many of Shakespeare's plays that it must have been close to his own. He presents the old law – which the Church itself still practises, despite the Gospels – as an ancient barbarity, the prime begetter of endless recurrences of tragedy. And in all his resolutions of tragedy he establishes its opposite: there is no salvation without creative mercy; and it is by the acceptance or rejection of love, deliberately, that the soul determines its own course – to cosmos or chaos, heaven or hell:

> Perdition catch my soul
> But I do love thee! and when I love thee not,
> Chaos is come again.

In *The Winter's Tale*, the trial theme is fully expanded. Leontes is particularly determined to cover his passions with the robe of justice. Hermione is tried in public. But Shakespeare, with his habitual subtlety, makes us see that, like the other heroes who passed sentences of death, Leontes is unconsciously trying himself and condemning himself. He says, ironically, to his wife:

> Your actions are my dreams;
> You had a bastard by Polixenes,
> And I but dream'd it. As you were past all shame,
> Those of your fact are so, so past all truth …

Every word of this – as he comes to realise later – is false of her and true of him. Under the sway of his passion, he is past shame and truth. But there is a terrible sincerity about him. So there was about Hamlet, Angelo and Othello: all of them, in the end, are past shame and truth; but they are not aware of it, because they have ceased to understand what these qualities mean. That a moral inversion must precede the tragic act is a principle from which Shakespeare never swerves. All the protagonists, like Hamlet, first induce madness in themselves; when they have done so, their fine speeches become meretricious, their golden-seeming words are merely glitter, and it is part of their tragedy to be self-deceived. Some of them achieve this so completely that they deceive the audience as well – a crowning irony from Shakespeare's point of view! Leontes, however, is transparent. No one can miss the point that the judge is pronouncing his own doom, when he says to the guiltless Hermione:

> ... so thou
> Shalt feel our justice, in whose easiest passage
> Look for no less than death.

At this point the messengers who had been sent to the oracle of Apollo return with the sealed scroll. It affirms, of course, Hermione's innocence; and it symbolises, as has been said, a message from the spirit to the passions. But Leontes' passion is still too furious to be ruled. He blasphemes the oracle:

> The sessions shall proceed: this is mere falsehood.

At once, a servant enters and announces that his son is dead. This sudden shock brings Leontes to the facing of the truth – which is essentially the truth about himself. We are instantly reminded of the shock-therapy of the Duke of Vienna, who faced his erring subjects with death in order to show them the true meaning of life. If a spiritual inversion led up to tragedy, then a spiritual reversion must take place before tragedy can be resolved. Shakespeare has several times shown us the one, and he is now – as in *Measure for Measure* – about to exhibit the other.

The queen faints, and is carried out. Then word is brought that she, too, is dead. She is not really dead; but she has planned to withdraw from the world for a time, and allow everyone, her husband especially, to suppose her to be dead. This double death-shock completes the spiritual awakening of Leontes. He sees his true self at last; and this, in Shakespeare's scheme, is the first step towards becoming 'man new made'.

He experiences a realisation of horror none the less – lashed by Paulina's tongue, as Othello was lashed by Emilia's. But he reacts quite differently from Othello – he is humble and utterly repentant. And instead of killing himself, he makes the far harder resolution to bear, himself, the public shame he would have inflicted on his wife:

> Prithee, bring me
> To the dead bodies of my queen and son:
> One grave shall be for both: upon them shall
> The causes of their death appear, unto
> Our shame perpetual. Once a day I'll visit
> The chapel where they lie, and tears shed there
> Shall be my recreation; so long as nature
> Will bear up with this exercise, so long
> I daily vow to use it. Come and lead me
> Unto these sorrows.

We may contrast this with the king's prayer in *Hamlet*:

> Try what repentance can: what can it not?
> Yet what can it, when one can not repent?
> O wretched state! O bosom black as death!
> O limed soul, that struggling to be free
> Art more engaged! Help, angels! make assay;
> Bow, stubborn knees; and heart with strings of steel
> Be soft as sinues of the new-born babe.
> All may be well.

It is now Shakespeare's purpose to show that if repentance is complete – that of Claudius did not go far enough – all will be well. But Shakespeare's optimism is by no means facile. We may remember the words spoken to Malcolm by Macduff:

> ... the queen that bore thee,
> Oft'ner upon her knees than on her feet,
> Died every day she liv'd.

And we are to assume that for the next sixteen years Leontes in the chapel will do the same. His way will not be easy.

It is now clear that Shakespeare is following a similar plan in *The Winter's Tale* to that which he adopted in *Measure for Measure*. Leontes, like Angelo, has been made to pass through every phase of the tragic sequence either actually or symbolically. He is morally guilty of the tragic act, he confesses to it, and believes it to have taken place. He knows that he deserves death; and he has accepted it, in the sense that he will die every day upon his knees. Symbolically speaking, one may say that the characters are dead: the baby Perdita exposed, the queen vanished, Leontes in the chapel – they are dead to the world. Shake-speare has again taken us along the road of tragedy, and led us to the gate of death: we are now to explore the opposite road, the way of rebirth.

The third act ends with the abandoning of Perdita on the desert 'coast' of Bohemia; and the storm which accompanies this gives us a last parallel with *Othello*. Shakespeare does not throw in storms haphazard; they are the physical counterparts of psychical conditions. And the storms which open the second act of *Othello* and close the third act of *The Winter's Tale* are the first and last gusts of a tempest of tragedy. In *Othello* we have the lines:

For do but stand upon the foaming shore,
The chidden billow seems to pelt the clouds;
The wind-shak'd surge, with high and monstrous mane
Seems to cast water on the burning Bear
And quench the guards of the ever-fixed Pole:
I never did like molestation view
On the enchafed flood

In *The Winter's Tale*, when Antigonus leaves Perdita to her fate, he says:

                    Blossom, speed thee well!
There lie, and there thy character ...

                              ... Farewell!
The day frowns more and more: thou'rt like to have
A lullaby too rough: I never saw
The heavens so dim by day. A savage clamour!

And as the fleet was sunk in *Othello*, so sinks the ship which brought Perdita to Bohemia. But this is the end of the tempest. The old shepherd takes up the baby 'for pity', and then says to his son, who has just watched the ship go down:

> Now bless thyself: thou mettest with things dying, I with things new-born.

There was a correspondence – and one significant contrast – between the allegorical figures grouped round Hamlet and Angelo; and this is also true of Othello and Leontes.

Desdemona is replaced by Hermione: love, which the tragic soul casts out. Cassio is represented by Polixenes: friendship which is, in intention, murdered. Emilia and Paulina are the lash of remorse, linked with the awakening of horror. The Duke of Venice and the oracle of Apollo are the voice of the spirit, recalling the soul to its own self. There is also the one arresting contrast; it is between the counsellors – Iago and Camillo.

When these corresponding figures are considered in conjunction with the series of parallel scenes, I think no one would maintain that such concinnity could be fortuitous.

The last words of the third act are from the old shepherd, now Perdita's foster-father, to his son:

'Tis a lucky day, boy, and we'll do good deeds on't.

II

Winter's Tale:
Resolution of the Tragedy

SIX YEARS (1604 to 1610), and eight plays, separate *Measure for Measure* from *The Winter's Tale*. It is remarkable how faithful Shakespeare remained to his principles both of philosophy and of construction. But the resolution of the tragedy is more fully elaborated and far more subtle in *The Winter's Tale*. The dramatic architecture of this play is complicated, and some of its elements must be considered in isolation before the full significance of the building becomes clear.

The fourth act takes place in Bohemia. Sixteen years have passed. Perdita has been brought up in the shepherd's cottage as a simple country maiden. Prince Florizel, son of King Polixenes, chances to see her and they fall in love. What relation their courtship has to the repentance of Leontes we will enquire later. But the first thing that is striking about this idyllic romance is that Shakespeare uses it to turn his tragic pattern inside-out. In place of the phases of tragedy, we find corresponding phases of regeneration; and this plan of construction, adumbrated in *The Winter's Tale*, is elaborated in *The Tempest*. Without doubt, a full sequence, balancing the nine phases of tragedy exactly, was in Shakespeare's mind; but he has only two acts in which to develop it here, and there is perhaps another reason why it is curtailed. We will examine the regeneration sequence first.

In the tragedies we were shown a fatal flaw in the hero's soul which made it impossible to resist the coming tempt-ation: now we are shown a principle of strength in the soul which enables the hero to triumph. In both cases there is some hint or characterisation of the tempter. In the first scene between Florizel and Perdita, she expresses her fear that King Polixenes will never allow him to marry a shep-herd's daughter:

> Even now I tremble
> To think your father, by some accident,
> Should pass this way as you did. O, the Fates!
> How would he look ...

Shakespeare frequently links fathers with the old law that must be transcended; and this is a hint of the temptation coming to Florizel, for he has already made Perdita a promise of true love:

> ... my desires
> Run not before mine honour, nor my lusts
> Burn hotter than my faith.

She, however, foresees a stern test, and answers:

> O, but, sir,
> Your resolution cannot hold, when 'tis
> Opposed, as it must be, by the power of the king:
> One of these two must be necessities,
> Which then will speak, that you must change this purpose
> Or I my life.

The pattern is taking shape. Opposing forces are about to fight in and for the soul – the king's power against fidelity to love; and there is to be no compromise. If the king wins, love will be cast out, and we shall be on the tragic path again; if he does not, the movement will be in the opposite direction. Although Polixenes is not, on the whole, a sinister figure, he is clearly characterised in this special context, as the voice of temptation. But now, in place of the flaw of the tragic heroes, Shakespeare displays to us a principle of strength. Florizel answers:

> Or I'll be thine, my fair,
> Or not my father's. For I cannot be
> Mine own, nor anything to any, if
> I be not thine. To this I am most constant,
> Though destiny say no.

There is a great deal more in this than a charming love-speech. Perdita, like the other heroines, is dual; she is herself, and she is Love. And Florizel is affirming the ethic which Shakespeare has established in the tragedies. The soul that rejects love is rejecting its own self; because its higher, or divine nature is love. The tragic heroes did not know this, or it would have saved them: each of them says, in effect, what Othello did – that his thoughts will never 'ebb to humble love'. It is part of Shakespeare's picture of the tragic inversion; for humble love is not an ebbing but a flowing of the tide of thought. Florizel is thus presented as the diametrical opposite of the tragic hero: he knows that to fail love is to fail himself, and to fail the world:

> For I cannot be
> Mine own, nor anything to any, if
> I be not thine.

The next statement is also foundational to Shakespeare's thought. He believes in destiny, which he often calls the stars or the Fates; but he does not believe that it is insuperable: again and again he proclaims that there is a spiritual principle in the soul which, if asserted with love and faith, is paramount. Fate would have brought *Measure for Measure* to a tragic close; but because virtue went forth from the duke, the conclusion was a triumph of love. And provided that Florizel does not falter, we are now promised a similar victory over the Fates:

> To this I am most constant,
> Though destiny say no.

He has no sooner said this than the king, who is to be the voice of his temptation – or perhaps, in this case, his testing would be a more appropriate phrase – enters in disguise.

Perdita then serves the guests; and here again Shakespeare is returning to his allegory of Love. She is a princess, who is thought to be a shepherd's daughter; for the festival, she is dressed as the goddess Flora; and she is the servant of them all. Shakespeare's deepest thought is always close to the spirit of the Gospels; and through whatever vesture he clothes his thought – classical, romantic, pastoral – the spirit shines. The gods themselves humble their deities to love.

In the tragic sequence there would now be a temptation, and a yielding. In the regenerative pattern there is a test, which is triumphantly passed. The king reveals himself:

> Mark your divorce, young sir,
> Whom son I dare not call; thou art too base
> To be acknowledged: thou a sceptre's heir,
> That thus affects a sheep-hook! ...

> If I may ever know thou dost but sigh
> That thou no more shalt see this knack, as never
> I mean thou shalt, we'll bar thee from succession ...

Polixenes strides away, without waiting for an answer; and it is to Perdita and her 'father' that Florizel replies:

> I am but sorry, not afeared; delay'd
> But nothing alter'd. What I was, I am.

This, from Shakespeare's pen, is the perfect answer. It expresses a thought that has reverberations in almost every play, and in the sonnets. 'I am that I am', and, conversely, ' I am not what I am'. They are the clearest indications that Shakespeare gives of the upward or downward movement of the soul. And the souls of Shakespeare's heroes are never static: their spiritual progress or degeneration is the true dynamic of Shakespearean drama.

In the tragedies, the next phase would be an inner conflict; and in contrast to this we are shown the calm assurance of a soul that is beginning to rise above the turmoil of the elements. To Perdita's fears for their future he says:

> It cannot fail but by
> The violation of my faith; and then
> Let nature crush the sides o' the earth together
> And mar the seeds within! Lift up thy looks ...

And in reply to Camillo, who tests him further, we see Florizel moving towards Shakespeare's proposition, again a distillation from the Gospels, that what matters is to gain the sovereignty of one's own soul, and that to exchange it for the kingdoms of the earth is to fall:

> Camillo,
> Not for Bohemia, nor the pomp that may

> Be thereat glean'd, for all the sun sees or
> The close earth wombs or the profound sea hides
> In unknown fathoms, will I break my oath
> To this my fair belov'd.

This is Shakespeare's way of rendering the rebuke to Satan; and it means that a soul has been tested, and triumphantly emerged.

If Shakespeare were reversing his tragic pattern completely – as he does in *The Tempest* – there would be a second test, and a second consolidation of the sovereignty within. But this is only sketched lightly in *The Winter's Tale*. In Act V, Scene i, there is a setback, a reversal of fortune, when, at what seems about to be the crowning moment, Florizel learns that his father is in close pursuit. This is hardly a test by Shakespeare's standards; but it is the outline of one, and proves that he was mindful of his constructional principles. For Florizel it is a moment of keen disappointment, and the manner in which he meets it shows that he has gone some way towards realizing the kingship of his soul and its dominion over fate. He says to Perdita:

> Dear, look up:
> Though Fortune, visible an enemy,
> Should chase us with my father, power no jot
> Hath she to change our loves.

Florizel has been described as 'the most poetically articulate of princely lovers', and certainly Perdita deserves to be praised no less, and yet, abruptly, from this point onwards, they are deliberately faded out. It is true that we may assume a union of love between them, and a triumph of the spirit – the climatic phases of the regenerative pattern; but these are not enacted; in fact, they would seem to be intentionally veiled. The young couple, whose love and courtship was so vividly created, do not exchange another word. They are eclipsed by their parents; and Shakespeare throws away a potentially magnificent scene of general reunion – resorting to the dramatist's most feeble expedient, reported speech – chiefly because Hermione could not have been there. Everything is sacrificed to Leontes and Hermione, that is, to the resolution of their tragedy; but the manner in which the young ones are disposed of is curious. Florizel's last words, which are in the first scene of the fifth act, are not to Perdita, but to Leontes:

> Beseech you, sir,
> Remember since you owed no more to time
> Than I do now: with thought of such affections,
> Step forth mine advocate ...

It is like a hint of identification, and a carrying back of Leontes to his own youth. And Perdita, in her last speech, has only one line to say; it is when she is gazing on the supposed statue of Hermione:

> So long could I
> Stand by, a looker on.

It is almost as if the young lovers were incorporated in the hero and heroine. Could there be more in this than a theatrical device? Shakespeare has such a predilection for double meanings that it is at least legitimate to consider the possibility of one here. He has been criticised for writing two plays in *The Winter's Tale*, and rolling them together somewhat loosely. But perhaps he intended them to be more closely integrated than they appear.

The second play, if one may call it that, begins in the fourth act. In discussing Shakespeare's last period, Tillyard* makes some interesting observations under the heading 'planes of reality'. May it be that the fourth act of *The Winter's Tale* is on a different 'plane of reality'? If so, then it would be natural, almost inevitable, for Shakespeare to conceive it allegorically. The theme of the play is the healing of the soul of Leontes, and he does not appear in the fourth act at all. Hamlet and Macbeth also step out of their respective plays for a considerable part of their fourth acts, but allegorically they are there. Could this be true of Leontes? If it were, then the courtship of Florizel and Perdita would not be something extraneous, but an integral part of the reconstruction of the hero's soul.

The fourth act is introduced by Time. The obvious purpose of Time's remarks is to explain the passage of sixteen years; but he says something significantly more:

> ... it is in my power
> To o'erthrow law, and in one self-born hour
> To plant and o'erwhelm custom.

What law is overthrown? Time is a measure of change; and time's law is evidently our common standard of measuring the succession of incidents in the physical world. But the same standard does not apply to psychical events, where the law may be said to be overthrown. What is a self-born hour? It could well be a period of inward or imaginative creation; and we have already seen that it is Shakespeare's contention that what the soul creates the world embodies. 'Custom' is presumably the course of

* Tillyard, *Shakespeare's Last Plays*.

events in the outer world, and this is either planted or overwhelmed, created or annihilated, in the 'self-born hour'. Can it be that this curious 'Bohemia', with a sea-coast, is really an inner world?

In the first short scene of Act I, we were told that visit-ors to Bohemia (and whatever else it may be, Bohemia is certainly the place of healing) will be given 'sleepy drinks'. Sleep is one of the ways of entry into the soul world – sleep, death and meditation. And in many passages Shake-speare associates healing with sleep; and, therefore, with a reconstruction in what we now call the unconscious. The tragic heroes are all debarred from this: they cannot sleep; their souls are in turmoil, and there is no peace in them. Brutus:

> Since Cassius first did whet me against Caesar,
> I have not slept.

Macbeth:

> Methought I heard a voice cry, 'Sleep no more!
> Macbeth does murder sleep', the innocent sleep,
> Sleep that knits up the ravell'd sleave of care,
> The death of each day's life, sore labour's bath,
> Balm of hurt minds, great nature's second course,
> Chief nourisher in life's feast ...

Iago, as he spies on Othello:

> Not poppy, nor mandragora,
> Nor all the drousy syrups of the world,
> Shall ever medecine thee to that sweet sleep
> Which thou ow'dst yesterday.

With all this, and more elsewhere, is it quite irrelevant that travellers to Bohemia – where there is balm for hurt minds, fresh nourishment for life, and pristine innocence – should be given 'sleepy drinks'? We might more easily think so were it not for Time's curious hint that the fourth act is on a different 'plane of reality', where his ordinary laws do not apply, and where events may be creations of the 'self-born hour'. This self-born hour, when the new is planted and the old is overwhelmed, is akin to a dream, yet something more; but in Shakespeare, dreams themselves are often something more. 'Your actions are my dreams.' Out of such dreams, events flow, as if from the womb of Time; and so, it seem to me, that what Shakespeare means by a self-born hour is a creative meditation.

Supposing that the fourth act were a creation of Leontes' dreams, that the line, 'Your actions are my dreams', continued to be true, what new planting, we may ask, had he proposed to himself at the end of the third act? When Hermione fainted and was carried out, but before he was told she was dead, Leontes promised that he would, 'new woo my queen'. And if Shakespeare had been intending to show this new wooing of Love in the soul as the means of its healing, he would have done so in an allegory. He does not state such ideas directly; but he projects them in an action that has a surface meaning which is adequate in itself at its own level, and an under-meaning for those who care to look. We have seen, in other plays, that the acceptance or rejection of love, is synonymous with health or sickness of the soul; and that events take place first in the soul, out of ordinary time, and are unfolded subsequently in the world.

Drawing these various strands together, it seems not impossible that the fourth act – so lovely in itself, yet seeming so tenuously linked with the first two – is an allegory of the healing of the tragic wound. I suggest that it is a reconstruction of Leontes' inner world, and takes place on a different plane of consciousness. He had sunk, ethically, through the temptations, to the act of darkness, of which he was morally guilty; then he sincerely repents.

'Try what repentance can.' Here is Shakespeare's answer. As Leontes is kneeling, day after day in the chapel, in contrition and tears, a new birth is taking place within him which is shown to us as an allegory in an idyllic world. In the guise of Florizel, he woos his lost wife again, in the person of Perdita, who is Hermione's second self. Again he, that is Florizel, is tempted to break faith; and again the agent of the temptation is Polixenes. But he has learnt by his experience of remorse and anguish; and this time he makes the perfect answer: 'I am nothing altered; what I was, I am.'

Leontes has now reversed the tragic sequence, and, in fact, the whole tragic pattern. The love which was lost, of which Perdita is the symbol, is received again, and he has 'brought water for his stain'. And if best men are moulded out of faults, he is not merely restored, but immeasurably better. When his re-creation – a word he uses of himself – is inwardly perfected, it may be outwardly expressed. The statue comes to life. And Florizel and Perdita slip back into their parents, like fresh perfections of their former selves, fated to excel them.

If this is the under-meaning of the fourth act – which would be consistent with Shakespeare's methods and philosophy – then it is as thoroughly integrated with the rest as is the play-within-the-play in *Hamlet*. But it is opposite in function, as it would have to be in a regener-ation sequence; the play scene in *Hamlet* is, allegorically, a pouring in of fresh poison as part of the soul's self-destruction, while the fourth act of *The Winter's Tale* is a process of self-healing by the balm of love.

Shakespeare is illustrating the upward path of the soul in contradistinction to the downward; and he does not do so vaguely, but by clothing definite ethical principles in action and poetry. There are moments when he seems to be feeling his way, moments that may be dramatic opportunism; but this only applies to the vesture of his thoughts, he is always quite clear about their ethical plan. The theme that man must be born again, in his own soul, is one of the threads that draw most of the religions of the world together; and it is doubtless a part of the spiritual ground on which all religions rest. This neogenesis is beautifully allegorised in *The Winter's Tale*, and perfectly in place there. Perdita's invocation to Proserpine comes when the inward creation is complete. Shakespeare surely knew what he was about when he made Love, seeking a new expression of itself, pray to the goddess of rebirth:

> O Proserpina,
> For the flowers now, that frighted thou let'st fall
> From Dis's waggon!

How marvellously apt to what has gone before, and what is to follow – like a rite performed in some other world, but linked in a chain of consequence with this; and the prayer is answered. Her lover has come back, and she garlands with him the flowers of a new spring.

This wonderful allegory – if such it is – of the healing of the tragic wound by love reveals Shakespeare as something more than a poet-philosopher; he appears as a physician of the soul. And it is perhaps worth noticing that the love-idyll in Bohemia begins and ends with a voyage. The sea is a universal symbol of the unconscious mind; and so it would seem as if, at the end of Act III, we sail into the world of the soul, and at the end of the fourth act we sail out again. I will not lay any weight on this point, however, because there are many voyages in Shakespeare that are not susceptible of such an interpretation, although some others might be. Nevertheless, it would not surprise me if Shakespeare knew more about psychoanalysis, under a different name, than our psychiatrists, or their patients, have yet dreamed of ; and it may well be that his deepest purpose in *The Winter's Tale* is to show how the outer life may be re-created from within.

12

There is Always a Choice

THE RESULTS of our enquiry into *Measure for Measure* and *The Winter's Tale* invite us to glance back at *Hamlet*. We have seen that the two main themes of the king's prayer in Hamlet have been elaborated in these later plays, and each has been shown leading to a solution of tragedy. Therefore, since Shakespeare wrote two plays out of the king's prayer, we cannot but suspect that he attributed special importance to the original scene.

The king was morally no worse than Angelo, who would have had Isabella's brother tortured to death, or Leontes, who commanded that his baby daughter be burnt alive; on the whole, indeed, he might seem the best of the three. We may, therefore, take it for granted that Shakespeare did not regard him as irredeemable. And we must give full weight to those good qualities in him which Hamlet, naturally, could not see, but which Shakespeare has been at pains to point out to us. Until the killing of Polonius – a point of no return for all the characters – we are meant to see the king as a 'limed soul struggling to be free', and to accord him our charity as such. He has not stifled his conscience, it is troubling him from the beginning; and although he is not prepared to shed the 'heavy burden' by relinquishing the fruits of his crime (few men would have been), short of that he is trying to make what amends he can; and his courtesy to Hamlet, in the first three acts, is not to be considered as duplicity. His prayer closes with the words, 'All may be well'. And since Shakespeare has demonstrated his ability to make all well for greater sinners, he could have done it here if he had wished. If he did not, it is not because the situation is intrinsically worse than, let us say, the casting away of Prospero and Miranda, or others that he has resolved, but because he wished to demonstrate the death-climax in *Hamlet*. But the fact that the king strove towards the light and failed, brings out this point: the play is his tragedy as well as Hamlet's. Shakespeare's sense of tragedy is different from the classical; what makes him care about his tragic characters is not that they *are* good, as Greek protagonists fundamentally are, but that they might have been.

Once we have made that point, we cannot but be struck by the correspondences that Shakespeare makes between Hamlet and the king. The king kills Hamlet's father, and, in Hamlet's exaggerated phrase, whores his mother. Hamlet kills Polonius, and, in his mind and speeches, whores his daughter. The king plots Hamlet's death by trickery. Hamlet, by the same trick, encompasses the death of two men. And lastly, their tragic courses converging, as it were, upon a single death-point, they kill each other. The fascination of this construction is that it reveals the mutual interaction for evil between two souls, which, nevertheless, both contain so much that is good.

If we see the king jet black and Hamlet snow white, we miss all this; and in doing so we lose an important part of

Shakespeare's meaning, which rests on the general analysis of the human soul as a battleground on which the
forces of light and darkness are contending, and where the
conflict ebbs and flows. It is this inner struggle that determines what is going to happen on the stage. And Shakespeare can turn the warfare to whatever outcome he
wishes for the culmination of a particular play. If an
upward-moving soul may suffer a tragic reverse, the converse is equally demonstrable. But, and this is of basic
importance, he never makes these reversals capriciously;
they are made according to his rules; and it is on his ethic,
ultimately, that his rules are founded.

We might ask ourselves at which point in Hamlet
Shakespeare could have reversed the tide of the inner
warfare if he had been intending, as he might have done,
to avert the tragic climax. This is not an idle speculation,
because Shakespeare himself must have made it when
working out the constructional problems of the resolution
for his later plays. Of one thing we may be positive – by
analogy with all the rebirth plays – if Shakespeare had
intended to regenerate Hamlet, he would have regener-
ated the king as well. When he decides on a resolution, he
does it thoroughly, and none of the sinning characters is
left out. 'Pardon's the word to all.'

Without going into the problem exhaustively, there are
two scenes in which – judged solely from the point of view
of Shakespeare's constructional principles – the opportunity to initiate a reversal of the deathward movement is
outstanding. The first is the nunnery scene (Act III, Scene
i). Just before Hamlet's dialogue with Ophelia, we have
the soliloquy of equipoise, 'To be, or not to be.' There are
moments when a hair may divide the false from the true,

and this is one. All hangs in balance, and nothing is irrevocable yet. Obviously, the dead king cannot be brought back to life; but the past – all the human past – is always and inevitably laden with crime, and there is a right and a wrong way of dealing with its consequence: that is the present question. What Hamlet is deciding here is Yes or No to life. First, he debates it in the abstract. Then he sees Ophelia, and the drama of the mind is embodied.

Writers of the snow-white Hamlet school have called this interview 'a trap'. But if we look carefully into the arranging of it – both in the previous part of the same scene and in Act II, Scene ii – we see that it was nothing of the sort. The king, the queen and Polonius, in these discussions, are all presented at their best. And immediately before it we have the king's aside, 'How smart a lash ...', which even his harshest critics have admitted to be a *cri de coeur*. There is no doubt that, at this juncture, they are united in the wish to be helpful to Hamlet. So far from being a trap, the meeting with Ophelia is an attempted rescue. And we are able to infer, from the allegorical content, that, had Shakespeare wished to reverse the death-trend, that is what it might have been. Ophelia reminds him of his love-gifts. He denies that he ever gave them. Then she says:

> My honour'd lord, you know right well you did;
> And with them words of so sweet breath composed
> As made the things more rich ...

Not only does he know it, but we know it; because Shakespeare has been careful to give us the evidence of his letter, closing with an eternal promise, 'I love thee best, O most best, believe it – thine evermore – Hamlet.' Now, he is faced with the moment of truth. And here, in strict accordance with his own rules, Shakespeare could have made a reversal; he would assuredly have done so, as elsewhere, by facing the hero suddenly with himself; and it would have followed, as the night the day, that he could not, then, have been false to that promise; he would have been compelled to turn in his tracks, and answer, in effect, like Florizel:

> Or I'll be thine, my fair,
> Or not my father's; for I cannot be
> Mine own, or anything to any, if
> I be not thine.

The quotation would have been most apt; for nothing and no one, at that moment, stood between Hamlet and Ophelia except his father's ghost. He had made a vow to Ophelia, 'thine evermore'. And he had taken an oath to the ghost, 'I have sworn't!' It is impossible to keep them both, and now he must decide. 'To be, or not to be ...' the oath to Love or the oath to Death – which? He dismisses Love to a nunnery, and keeps his appointment with Death. But it would not have been impossible, on analogy with the plays of resolution, for Shakespeare to have changed the direction here. If Hamlet had made Florizel's reply, and that other:

> It cannot fail but by
> The violation of my faith ...

then, if we see Ophelia in the full significance of her stature as the allegory of Love, a life-trend would have been initiated at this point. Hamlet's later diabolical soliloquy, 'Now I could drink hot blood', would have been impossible if he had kept his oath to Love; and he would therefore have been in a position to have dealt creatively instead of destructively with the king and queen. He very nearly succeeds in dealing successfully with the queen as it is – 'O, Hamlet, thou hast cleft my heart in twain.' And in the previous scene we have been shown the king on his knees, his heart almost cleft in twain.

This brings us to the scene of the king's prayer, which, I am sure, had a central importance in Shakespeare's eyes; for not only did he elaborate its themes later, as we have already noticed, but also the essential situation is one that he repeats. It is a situation, I think, that imprints itself very strongly in the memory of a theatre audience: the kneeling sinner, and behind him the standing figure with the naked rapier of retribution. And we find it closely paralleled in the regeneration plays: Angelo on his knees before the duke, Iachimo at the feet of Posthumus, Alonso and Antonio at Prospero's mercy. In each instance, an act of creative mercy gave passage to the flow of 'power divine', which is the real agent of regeneration.

Shakespeare might then, by adherence to his own rules, have made *Hamlet* into a regeneration play, including, of course, the king and queen. And it seems certain that he would have done so by reversing Hamlet's direction in the nunnery scene. It would not have been necessary to alter the king and queen; because, until the death of Polonius, both of them are tending to move in the right way. It is Hamlet who is moving downwards, as indeed he never ceases to do, and for that reason it is impossible for him to be a channel of spiritual power. If he had been, the king's prayer would have been answered, as if by heaven, through Hamlet; but there was no agent through which heaven could work; and the divine work is done, in this world, by embodied souls or not at all.

> He, who the sword of heaven will bear
> Should be as holy as severe ...

Hamlet was not holy; and he was therefore unable to bear the sword of justice in the right way. The whole play, as I said before, is a challenge to our preconceptions of what justice really is. Had the king been faced with what we might call Shakespearean justice, there is no reason why he should not have followed Leontes to the chapel of expiation, raised a like monument 'unto our shame perpetual', and died every day upon his knees, to be reborn. And that, probably, would have been the best form of spiritual easement to the ghost in his 'prison house', for his soul-state was certainly not bettered by the multiple murders to which his visitation led.

Some readers will be thinking, no doubt, that any suggestions for giving *Hamlet* a 'happy ending' are frivolous. I think not, for the reason that they are likely to have visited Shakespeare's mind, and it is worth while to try and follow his thought. Of course, he never intended *Hamlet* to be anything but a death-play. But it is equally certain that he must have been greatly exercised, at this time, with the technical problems – which are anything but simple – of presenting regeneration on the stage, because he made the attempt in his next play, *Measure for Measure*. Perhaps he was not satisfied with that, and left the question in the recesses of his mind for some years, until he found fresh answers to it near the end of his career. In dramatic terms, the answers are not perfect, and have been much misunderstood; but it is a problem of such magnitude that no playwright since, except Goethe, has even faced it, or, for that matter, recognised that it exists.

Before leaving *Hamlet*, it should be reaffirmed that, in Shakespeare's ethic, the sinning world can be healed only if the sinning souls in it are healed. He shows that the soul may be in a state equivalent to 'hell'; but he does not accept the doctrine of eternal damnation. He distinguishes between the doer and the act. This point is raised in *Measure for Measure*. To Angelo, it seems absurd to condemn the crime but not the criminal. Shakespeare takes the opposite view, believing that a course of action can always, in this world or another, be reversed – and will be. And Shakespearean justice might be defined as the study and application of the means to bring this reversal about.

There is some comfort, then, for those who see regeneration in Hamlet, or in any other of Shakespeare's sinners. But they look for it in the wrong place. It is of the utmost importance to see that Hamlet did evil; the meaning of the death-climax, and therefore of the whole tragedy as Shakespeare conceived it, is lost to us without that. But it does not damn Hamlet permanently, nor anyone else. Shakespeare's ethic of redemption is not worked out in this play; but Hamlet's personal redemption is, I believe, foretold. I would not, however, attempt to prove this. I merely put it forward on the flimsy grounds that I feel it to be so. But since there is undoubtedly a spiritual side to Shakespeare's plays, and he treats his characters with the conviction that they are 'nurslings of immortality', he certainly held some view of Hamlet's wider destiny. I find it, though I do not presume to suppose that others will agree, in his epitaph, sung, as it surely ought to be, by Ophelia:

> How should I your true love know
> > From another one?
> > By his cockle hat and staff,
> > > And his sandal shoon.

This has nothing to do with Polonius. In reality, she is singing about her own true love, of whose identity no one is in doubt. He is to set out on a pilgrimage of expiation, with his cockle hat, his staff and his sandal shoon. The cockle hat was worn by medieval pilgrims who were about to cross the sea, to the shrine of Compostella, to obtain forgiveness. It might well be that the sea is the waters of death; and beyond them, perhaps, is a holier shrine. And so I take this to be Shakespeare's valediction to a pilgrim soul,

> Which bewept to the grave did not go
> > With true-love showers.

'I hope all will be well. We must be patient, but I cannot choose but weep.'

13

Passion Plays and other Parallels

THE LOVE-TRAGEDIES – *Romeo and Juliet*, *Troilus and Cressida* and *Antony and Cleopatra* – present, I think, special problems; and I hope to make this group the subject of a further study. *King Lear* also demands a different approach, which I must defer. But analysis of all the plays we have so far considered has shown us some stable elements in Shakespeare's construction not previously suspected; and to three of these, he himself would seem to have attributed special importance.

> FIRST: Two temptations, or tests of the soul (he doubtless envisaged a series of them in the natural course of a life), which serve as a spiritual ladder that may be – must be – either mounted or descended. Facing and replying to these tests constitute the critical moments of decision, from which the climax logically follows.
>
> SECOND: The soul is like a kingdom in which the true self should reign, by divine right; but until this happens, it is a battleground; and Shakespearean drama is ultimately this inner warfare projected on to the stage.

THIRD: The powers engaged in the interior struggle are personified; so that the characters grouped round the hero are both real – that is, characters in their own right – and allegorical figures at the same time.

Shakespeare did not invent these elements; they all existed in the drama and poetry of the Middle Ages; but he refined and united them into what is, surely, the most elaborate and fascinating theory of dramatic construction that has ever been evolved. He could hardly have done so in isolation. There must have been a circle who understood his constructional principles and the under-meaning of his plays; but the prosecution of Marlowe and Sir Walter Raleigh for 'atheism' would have forced its members to secrecy. We must also remember that the period, like the Middle Ages, delighted in mysteries for their own sake; every guild was a 'mystery', and its secrets, whether valuable or not, were held inviolable. The closing of the theatres during the Commonwealth caused a break in the English dramatic tradition; and during this time, pre-sumably, the Shakespearean secrets were totally lost.

We must now enquire where Shakespeare found seed-ideas of these three principles.

The Reformation in England did not put an end to the production of the old religious dramas, and Shakespeare must have seen some of these performed. The medieval stage, even when it was a movable pageant, was essentially triple; whether it was a grandiose construction as at Valenciennes, or a makeshift of the market place, it had to accommodate action in the three divisions of the theological universe – earth, heaven and hell. Earth, of course, was the centre of dramatic interest; but each actor made his last exit to join God or the devil. The old plays did not end on a note of interrogation, they decided the eternal destiny of souls; and various devices were used to represent the extra-mundane destinations. There might be an over-stage, for example, where sat God and the angels, and a kind of cellarage, furnished with fire, the devil and the demons. The expedients were many, the principle one; and the most constant, as it was the most fearsome piece of scenery, was a cavernous opening, to the left of God, representing the mouth of hell. From the stage proper, where the world-drama was enacted, the souls of the characters joined, as it were, alternative processions, one ascending to heaven and the other going down into the pit. The impression so created was probably both crude and strong.

On a spectator of Shakespeare's sensibility, the effect of such productions must have been twofold: he would have felt their philosophical inadequacy and their dramatic power. But when combined with the five-act classical construction, which was derived mainly from Roman comedy by way of medieval commentaries on Terence, they offered a splendid foundation to build upon. The old Morality Plays are sometimes spoken of as dull; if they were, the fault was in the authors and not the form. C.S. Lewis* has saved from oblivion the nightmare of a seventh-century monk, in which he dreamed that his soul left his body and that the powers of heaven and hell fought for its possession, while his own virtues and vices, realistically personified, joined the opposing forces, the one group taunting and the other exhorting him. The monk's dream was, in

* Lewis, *The Allegory of Love*, p.86.

effect, a Morality Play; and so far from being dull that the poor man awoke in a sweat of terror. In fact, the dramatic potential of these plays, springing from a deep stratum of the unconscious, was very great, but it was usually dissipated by their inordinate length and prolixity.

Shakespeare must have pondered the old drama, and then reshaped it. The rebirth of the five-act form helped to concentrate its power, and the tide of opinion flowing against the orthodox theologians assisted him to refashion its philosophy. The tendency of renaissance thought towards syncretism, corresponding with his natural gifts, at length enabled him to present the *philosophia perennis** and the higher morality of the Gospels in complete accord. This gave him a faith, not tied in the old wine-skin of ecclesiasticism, but fresh from the chalice of reason and love.

The five-act form, though valuable, was not everything. Without it, the old plays were still dramatically strong: if they had been unable to move an audience, they would not have lived for centuries. Shakespeare must have appreciated this quality; and whatever he admired, he set out to enhance. I suggest that he did so by translating the material construction of the medieval stage into the intellectual structure of his own work. His protagonists, to take a single example, always belong to one 'procession' or the other, heaven-bound or hell-bound, and he is never in doubt as to whether they are moving up or down.

The mouth of hell, with its flickering fires, was ever open in the old religious dramas, with the devil and his minions constantly coming in and out. To the literally

---

* 'Perrenial philosophy.' The sixteenth-century idea that there is a perennial truth expressed in all philosophies and religions regardless of their cultural pedigree.

minded, in an age when torture was still in legal use, this must have been horrific. And the actors in the down-going stream would assuredly have displayed a realisation of horror on this appalling threshold. This mime at hell's mouth is quite likely to have been the basis of Shakespeare's eighth phase of tragedy – the realisation of horror, which is subsequent to crime and precedent to death:

> O! cursed, cursed slave. Whip me, ye devils,
> From the possession of this heavenly sight!
> Blow me about in winds! roast me in sulphur!
> Wash me in steep-down gulfs of liquid fire!

Surely, Shakespeare is suiting words to actions he has seen portrayed – possibly the last ravings of a Herod. If so, it means that his conception of tragedy is in arresting contrast to that of the Greeks. In Classical tragedy, the hero's sufferings have a purifying quality; and there is a strong intimation of bliss to come or apotheosis. In Shakespeare this is not so. He shows us a clear path to bliss and apotheosis. It does not lead through 'steep-down gulfs of liquid fire'. It leads away from them. The soul may enter it by joining the ascending procession; and this is done by making the correct answer in the critical scenes of temptation. That is why these scenes are of cardinal importance in Shakespeare's dramatic pattern: they are rungs in an ethical ladder, to mount or descend; and the direction of movement may at any time be reversed, by compliance with conditions that are lucidly defined.

A correct answer, in its special context, may be far from perfect; but it must be concordant with an ideal. And if we ask what is the perfect answer to the temptations, then we must look, as Shakespeare indubitably did, to ideal examples. Christ and the Buddha were both tempted, and it is relevant to consider their replies.

The temptations of both were in principle the same: they were tempted to subordinate the spiritual to the material. 'Command this stone that it be made bread!' It sounds innocent; but it has a subtle under-meaning, 'Confess your dependence on the physical world.' And so the perfect answer is to affirm that the new life, the life of the resurrection, is not dependent, but is nourished by the spirit. 'All the kingdoms of the earth will I give thee.' There is nothing inherently wrong in earthly kingship; none the less, the perfect answer is to assert sovereignty in the heavenly kingdom which lies within.

The temptations of the Buddha, in the night of storm before his enlightenment, were more numerous and complex; but they were essentially the same. Mara tempted him with lust, to which the absolute supremacy of the Nirvanic bliss is the perfect reply. Having failed, Mara tried the opposite – pain. Still, the answer is an affirmation of the spirit: the weapons of the fiends were not deflected, but transmuted into a rain of flowers.

The host of Mara hastening, as arranged, each one exerting his utmost force, taking each other's place in turns, threatened every moment to destroy him,   1079
Fiercely staring, grinning with their teeth, flying tumultuously, bounding here and there; but Bodhisattva, silently beholding them, watched them as one would watch the games of children;   1080
Their flying spears, lances and javlins stuck fast in space, refusing to descend; the angry thunder-drops and mighty hail, with these, were changed into the five-coloured lotus flowers,   1082

But not a hair of his was moved, and Mara's host was filled
with sorrow. Then in the air the crowd of angels, their forms
invisible, raised their voices: saying: 1087
'Let go your foul and murderous thoughts against that silent
Muni, calmly seated! You cannot with a breath move the
Sumeru mountain;   1089
'Lust, hate and ignorance, these are the rack and bolt, the
yoke placed on the shoulder of the world; through ages long,
he has practised austerities to rescue men from these their
fetters,   1102
'Though all the earth were moved and shaken, yet would this
place be fixed and stable; him, thus fixed and well-assured,
think not that you can overturn.'*   1104

The life of the Buddha would not have been known to
Shakespeare. But there can be no doubt that the temptations in the Gospels – both the resistances of Christ and
the yieldings of Judas – were at the heart of his tragic
pattern. And the ideal standard, by which his protagonists
are measured in their temptations, is the highest religious
ethic of both East and West. The perfect answer is always
an assertion of the sovereignty of the spirit. Shakespeare
expresses this in a principle from which he never swerves:

This above all: to thine own self be true.

We may take this on the surface, or in depth. Understood
in depth, it implies some mystical insight into the nature
of the self.† Many people have this to some extent; and
the careful cultivation of it, the striving to know oneself,
is another Shakespearean principle. The Duke of Vienna
and Prospero, having begun to study themselves, had

* *The Sacred Books of the East*, Vol. XIX, edited by Max Müller. Oxford, 1883.
† See Jung, *Psychology and Alchemy*, Collected Works, Vol. XII, p.18.

caught at least a glimpse of the divine immanence, and therefore they had spiritual power.

The old drama must have seemed to Shakespeare a right pattern imperfectly understood; for he uses the pattern, and, by placing it in the context of the Perennial Philosophy, gives it a universal interpretation. At the same time, he maintains the union of religion with the theatre; because temptation scenes are at the centre of both the religious and dramatic suspense, and the fate of the soul and the plot of the play flow from them alike. We now see that the ethical question with which we began, 'What ought the hero to do?', so far from being irrelevant is the pivot on which the action turns. The hero is compelled to make an ethical decision; and this determines the direction that he and the plot itself will take.

Our best example of traditional medieval drama, still holding a vast modern audience, is the Ober-Ammergau Passion Play;* and when we study this from the constructional point of view, some striking correspondences with the Shakespearean pattern come to light. After Christ, Judas is by far the most dramatic character in the play, and the more we examine this medieval presentation of Judas, the more it looks like a paradigm of Shakespeare's tragic sequence.

In the first act of the *Passion Play* we are shown the traders, whom Christ drives from the temple, and the priests, who are in league with them. These two groups are characterised as the enemies of Christ; and each, in turn, is afterwards a voice of temptation to Judas.

* *The Passion Play at Ober-Ammergau*, translated by Maria Trench. Kegan Paul, 1910.

In Act III, Scene iii,we are shown the flaw in Judas's soul. Christ's feet have been anointed with the precious ointment, and Judas exclaims:

> To pour away such costly ointment! What waste!
> *Christ:* Friend Judas, look me in the face! Waste on Me, thy Master?
> *Judas:* I know that Thou lovest not useless expense. The ointment might have been sold and the poor thereby supported.
> *Christ:* Judas, lay thy hand upon thy heart. Is it only sympathy for the poor which so greatly moves thee?
> *Judas:* Three hundred pence at least could have been got for it. What a loss for the poor, and for us.

Love of money is the weak spot which the temptations will probe, and this is suggested again by Judas's soliloquy, Act IV, Scene iii. Judas:

> Wherefore should I follow him? ... His great works give hope that he will again raise up the kingdom of Israel; but He seizes not the opportunities which offer themselves. ... There is nothing in prospect with Him, except approaching poverty and humiliation, and, instead of the expected participation in His kingdom, persecution, perchance, and prison. I will withdraw myself. Happily, I was always provident, and have laid aside a little here and there out of the bag.

In the next scene, the traders tempt him. He tells them the story of the costly ointment, and they exclaim:

> And thou canst yet be friends with Him? Thou oughtest to take thought for thine own future, were it only now.
> *Judas:* I am thinking of it even now. But how to find a good livelihood at once?
> *Dathan:* Thou needest not long seek that ...

They tell him of the reward offered by the High Priest's Council. He yields to this first temptation; and the next scene is a soliloquy of inner conflict:

> My word is given. I shall not rue it. Shall I, forsooth, go out of the way of approaching good fortune? ... Judas, thou art a prudent man ... yet I am afraid to come before the Master. I shall not be able to bear His piercing glance, and my companions will see in my face that I am a – No! that I will not be, I am no traitor! What am I doing except showing the Jews where the Master is to be found? That is no betrayal; more is needed for that. Away with these fancies! Courage, Judas, thy livelihood is at stake!

In Act VI, Scene ii, he is again tempted to the betrayal; this time, it is by the council of the priests. He is in conflict, now, and wavering. A Rabbi enters, with the money:

> Come, Judas, take the thirty pieces of silver, and be a man! (*He reckons them to him on a small stone table, so that they fall with a sharp sound; Judas sweeps them eagerly into his bag.*)

Act VIII, Scene iv, is the act of darkness. Judas betrays Christ by a kiss.

Then comes a realisation of horror, in two soliloquies; the first is Act IX, Scene v:

> Fearful forebodings drive me hither and thither. That word in the house of Annas – He must die! O that word pursues me everywhere! No! they will not, they will not carry it so far! It were horrible – and I – the guilt of it! Here in the house of Caiaphas I will enquire how matters stand. Shall I go in? I can no longer bear them, these uncertainties, and I am terrified of attaining certainty, but it must come some time.

And the second, Act X, Scene i:

> My fearful foreboding has then become a horrible cer-
> tainly, Caiaphas has condemned the Master to death. ...
> It is over! no hope, no deliverance left. If the Master had
> willed to save Himself, He would have made them feel
> His might a second time in the garden. Now He will do
> it no more. And what can I do for Him, I, miserable I,
> who have delivered Him into their hands? They shall have
> the money again – the blood money: they must give me
> my Master back again! Yet – will he be saved thereby?
> O vain hope! They will scorn me, I know it! Accursed
> synagogue! thou hast seduced me through thy messen-
> gers, hast hidden thy bloody design from me until thou
> hadst Him in thy clutches. I will have no part in the blood
> of the Innocent!

Finally, Act X, Scene vii, is death. Judas enters, alone:

> Whither shall I go to hide my infamy? No forest darkness
> is secret enough, no rocky cavern deep enough! Swallow
> me up, O earth! Alas, my Master, best of all men, have
> I sold – delivered Him up to ill-treatment, to the most
> agonizing death! How gracious was He even towards me!
> How He comforted me when gloomy misery often
> oppressed my soul! How lovingly did He remind me and
> warn me, even when already I brooded over my treachery.
> Execrable covetousness, thou alone hast seduced me! Alas,
> now no longer a disciple, never dare I come again into the
> presence of one of the brethren. An outcast – everywhere
> hated and abhorred even by those who led me astray –
> I wander about alone with this glowing fire in my heart!
> Alas, if I could only dare again to behold His countenance,
> I might cling to Him, the only anchor of hope! but he lies
> in prison, is perchance already put to death through the
> fury of His enemies – ah no! through my guilt! Woe is me

— me, the offscouring of mankind! For me there is no hope, my crime can no longer be repaired by any penitence! He is dead, and I am His murderer! Unhappy hour, when my mother bore me! Shall I any longer bear these tortures? No, I will not go a step further! Here will I breathe thee out, accursed life! Let the most miserable of all fruit hang on this tree! (*He tears off his girdle.*) Ha! come, thou serpent, twist round me! strangle the traitor! (*He prepares for suicide. The curtain falls.*)

The construction of the *Passion Play*, so far as the role of Judas is concerned, might have been drafted by Shakespeare; but this is a traditional Judas of the medieval stage. Eight of Shakespeare's nine phases of tragedy are clearly exhibited. And we may notice that Judas is not entirely bad; the priests, for instance, are worse. I do not think we need look further for the origin of Shakespeare's tragic pattern. All his doomed heroes sin in the same way — they betray the Best. They betray the immanent divinity in themselves.

There are also three trial scenes in the *Passion Play*. Christ is brought before Caiaphas, Pilate and Herod. Each of these judges represents an aspect of the generally accepted contemporary law; yet in every case, it is the law, and not the accused, that is guilty. We have sufficiently examined a few of Shakespeare's trial scenes for it to be unnecessary to expatiate further on the parallel. In *Measure for Measure*, Angelo says:

> It is the law, not I condemn your brother.
> ... he must die to-morrow.

And in the *Passion Play*, Act IX, Scene iii, Caiaphas says:

He has unanimously been declared guilty of death. Yet not I, and not the Sanhedrim, but the law of God itself declares the judgment of death upon Him.

All the learned doctors of the law agree. What, then, is justice? That is, perhaps, the basic question of Shakespeare's tragedies. And every one of them, especially *Hamlet*, is a challenge to our preconceptions.

14

The Soul as a Kingdom

AS THE ACTORS in the down-going stream showed
horror at hell's mouth, so those who reached the
'gate of heaven' would naturally exhibit joy. All
writers have found it easier to depict crime and horror
than well-doing and bliss. Shakespeare is no exception.
But quite early in his career (1594) we may sense the 'gate
of heaven' in the dying speech of Richard II:

> Mount, mount, my soul! thy seat is up on high,
> Whilst my gross flesh sinks downward, here to die.

These last words of Richard bring us to the second of
Shakespeare's elements: the idea of the soul as a kingdom
in which the true self should be enthroned. Shortly before
Richard rose to what is at least an approach to a realisation of heaven, his long soliloquy tells us that the kingship
of his own soul is what he is pathetically struggling to
attain. And the implication would seem to be that because
he made this attempt, which was right, therefore he
achieved the heavenly confirmation at his death. The
whole speech merits most careful study as a foreshadowing
of Shakespeare's method in later plays, where the inner
dramas at which Richard hints are actually staged.

I have been studying how I may compare
This prison where I live unto the world:
And for because the world is populous,
And here is not a creature but myself,
I cannot do it; yet I'll hammer it out.
My brain I'll prove the female to my soul;
My soul the father: and these two beget
A generation of still-breeding thoughts,
And these same thoughts people this little world,
In humours like the people of the world,
For no thought is contented. ...
Thus play I in one person many people,
And none contented: sometimes I am king;
Then treason makes me wish myself a beggar,
And so I am: then crushing penury
Persuades me I was better when a king:
And I am king'd again ...

Richard, and perhaps Shakespeare also, is feeling his way
through a twilight of self-knowledge, in the right direction. It was with similar meditations, we may reasonably
suppose, that the Duke of Vienna and Prospero began the
study of themselves. But this speech was written about
seventeen years before Shakespeare created Prospero; and
if he himself practised introspection for so long (the passage is clearly the fruit of some personal experiment), and
if he had even half the gift for it that he had for poetry, he
must have come to his final plays with a sound knowledge
of psychoanalysis. The seed of this idea he may also have
found in the old religious drama; for the conflict in the
soul was the subject of the Morality Plays, where it is
exhibited by the aid of simple, rather crude allegorical
figures. Shakespeare's allegory, with its extraordinary

subtlety, owed something to the Moralities, but it is worlds beyond them.

Rulership of the inner kingdom, truth to oneself and sovereignty of spirit are three phases, three dressings of thought, for a single intuition. And this psychological experience, however variously arrayed in words, is one of the habitual discoveries of deep introspection. Shakespearean and Buddhist temptation scenes, without any conscious connection, are measurable by one standard. And Shakespeare's intuition of the inner kingdom, its conflict and its pacification, has similar confirmations of universality. That it should harmonise with the text, 'The kingdom of heaven is within you', is, of course, intended; but that it should have found almost identical expression in the mysticism of China, of which no sixteenth-century European knew anything, shows that it is not an embroidered blossom, but the flower of a living seed. This correspondence is pertinent to Shakespearean ethics; but I will not, now, pursue it further than a brief quotation from *The Secret of the Golden Flower*:

> The lower heart moves like a strong, powerful commander who despises the Heavenly Ruler because of his weakness, and has seized for himself the leadership of the affairs of state. But when the primordial castle can be fortified and defended, then it is as if a strong and wise Ruler sat upon the throne. ... When the Ruler at the centre is thus in order, all those rebellious heroes will present themselves with lances reversed ready to take orders.*

It is important to notice that not only is the imagery

* *The Secret of the Golden Flower*, translated by R. Wilhelm, with commentary by C.G. Jung.

similar, but so also is the nature of the victory: the 'rebel-lious heroes' are not destroyed, but given perfect employ-ment; in the same way, the weapons of the fiends were not annihilated by the Buddha, but transformed; and the Shakespearean ethic, whether applied to the inner world or the outer, is in conformity with this; condemnation and destruction are never presented as the right solution, but always creative mercy, which includes mercy to oneself. An essential part of the regeneration of Leontes, after his full repentance, is:

> At the last,
> Do as the heavens have done, forget your evil;
> With them forgive yourself.

All must be forgiven, because none is without fault:

> O! think on that,
> And mercy then will breathe within your lips,
> Like man new made.

We uncover, here, a common objective – Shakespearean, Christian, Buddhist, Taoist – *man new made*, first within and then without. And it is because the ideal is the same that the ethic which leads to it is similar.

We now come to the third element: Shakespeare's allegorical construction. In his soliloquy, Richard finds, or breeds within himself, a fully populated world; and it is the interrelation of these thought-children, their har-monies and discords, which determines the state of his soul. Shakespeare, by means of his dual characters, put these thought-children on the stage, and we see the strife in the hero's soul enacted before us. The first sentence quoted above from *The Secret of the Golden Flower* could be the abstract of a tragedy and its resolution, and is not unreminiscent of *The Tempest*, a preliminary usurpation, and a final victory for the rightful ruler.

Once again, the seed-idea of this principle of construction was not of Shakespeare's own conceiving: it was an inheritance from medieval poetry, and in particular from that part of *Le Roman de la Rose* composed by Guillaume de Lorris. I do not know if Shakespeare read French, but he certainly read Chaucer's translation, *The Romaunt of the Rose*, which had its first printing in 1532. In this beautiful flower of the Middle Ages, the lover, in his courtship, encounters a number of people, some helpful and some not, who are in reality moods and qualities of the lady herself. By Bialacoil (*Bel Accueil*), for example, he is greatly assisted:

> I sawe come with a gladde chere
> To me a lusty bachelere
> Of good stature and of good hight
> And Bialacoil forsoth he hight
> Sone he was to Curtesy
> And he me graunted ful gladly
> The passage of the vtter hay
> And sayd/sir: howe that ye may
> Passe if your wyl be
> The fresshe Roser for to se ...*   2981-89

Bialacoil is the gracious reception, child of her good manners, who is second nature to the lady; and he is a great help to the lover, allowing him to pass easily through the 'vtter hay', outer hedge, and to glimpse the Rose, which is the symbol of her love. But the lady is not all sugar and spice. Daungere (*Danger*) is a tempestuous mood of rebuff:

* *Chaucer Society Texts*, First Series, LXXXII.

> With that anone sterte out Daungere
> Out of the place where he was hydde
> His malyce in his chere was kydde
> Ful great he was and blacke of hewe ...   3130-33

When this monster springs upon him, the lover is put to flight!

> I durst no more make there abode
> For the chorle he was so wode
> So ganne he thretto and manace
> And through the haye he dyd me chace
> For feare of him I trymbled and quoke
> So chorlisshly his heed he shoke ...   3159-64

And so a whole company of moods and qualities not only affect the lover, represent the lady, and dramatise the courtship, but are also characterised as individuals and carry on a play among themselves. It is a form of psycho-analysis, not in the service of science but of art. Shakespeare had only to carry this method of construction a step further, to mask the allegory completely by replacing symbolic with realistic names, in order to be able to write two plays in one – a surface drama which would appeal to everyone, and an under-drama expressing his deepest thoughts to a circle of the select. From Guillaume de Lorris, probably, he learnt one of the most subtle secrets of his art.

If this kind of construction seems artificial to us, that is only because we have ceased to be familiar with allegory at all. Even a little systematic introspection will prove to anyone that he has within him many 'selves', which, or who, when circumstances favour them, will appear, and either take command or strive for it, with astonishing vitality. It is by no means unnatural to picture the ' I', or centre of self-consciousness, as a king surrounded by a populous and often turbulent court. And until these sub-selves are tried by the test of circumstance, their true power or even their existence may be unknown. Many people have been astonished by their own conduct – either for better or for worse – in an unprecedented situation.

In his commentary on *The Secret of the Golden Flower*, Jung writes:

> If the unconscious figures are not accorded the dignity of spontaneously effective factors, one becomes the victim of a one-sided belief in the conscious, which finally leads to a state of mental tension. Catastrophies are then bound to occur, because despite all one's consciousness, the dark psychic powers have been overlooked. It is not we who personify them; *they have a personal nature from the very beginning.**

The importance of the *Roman de la Rose* is partly this: Guillaume de Lorris is the first poet deliberately to clothe the inner population with personality and to present its activities as a drama in the outer world. He had, of course, many imitators – some of whom were extremely dull and clumsy; but Shakespeare bettered his instruction. He produced a fusion of realism and allegory in which there are not only dual characters, but also a dual plot. The fourth act of *The Winter's Tale*, for example, is acceptable at two different levels – objective and subjective – in the same sense that Daungere, in the *Romance of the Rose*, may be taken as either a swarthy villain, leaping from an ambush on the unsuspecting lover, or as the lady's most unpleasant mood. But if we ask, What is the full *significance* of

* *Op. cit.*, p.119.

Daungere, of Ophelia, or of the fourth act of *The Winter's Tale?* – we must then proceed, through an analysis of the realistic and allegorical components separately, to an integration of the two. Poetry and drama of this kind can only be the fruit of much introspection, along the lines of Richard's soliloquy; and the fact that the integration, the union of the inner and the outer, is reminiscent of certain types of mystical experience may not be irrelevant. It also leads to a genuine exploration of the unconscious.

In reviewing Shakespeare's many examples of dual characters, three types seem to be outstanding. First is the beautiful young woman who symbolises Love – Ophelia, Mariana, Desdemona, Hermione, Perdita. Second is the aged counsellor symbolizing Fidelity – Polonius, Escalus, Camillo, Gonzalo. Third is the personified fault in the hero's soul, of which Iago is a clear instance. The resemblance between these and the principle archetypes that Jung has found in the unconscious cannot but give one pause. In Jung's terminology, they are the Anima, the Wise Old Man and the Shadow. According to him, these archetypes exist in us all; they frequently appear in dreams, and always at some point in the course of a full analysis.

The interrelation of the archetypes, as revealed by psychoanalysis, is often suggestive of Shakespeare's methods. When, for instance, the Anima in her fair aspect is repressed, the dark forces of the unconscious present her destructive counterpart (Mariana pleading for life, replaced by Isabella clamouring for death), or by a similar inversion process, the pure sweetheart or wife is conceived and treated as a harlot. In *An Introduction to Jung's Psychology*, Frieda Fordham says of the Anima: 'She is also two-sided or has two aspects ... on the one hand the pure, the good, the noble, goddess-like figure, on the other the prostitute, the seductress or the witch. It is when a man has repressed his feminine nature, when he under-values feminine qualities or treats women with contempt, that this dark aspect is most likely to present itself.' Shakespeare has staged this in his allegory of the rejection of Love as the cause or pre-requisite of tragedy; and the principle of psychic inversion is one of the most important elements in his technique.

What Jung calls the Shadow is the personification of the dark side of the soul; it is a residue of primitive impulse and barbarous desire which is repressed, because it is incompatible with civilised conduct, but not dissipated. Jung says of the Shadow that it is – 'a moral problem which challenges the whole ego personality'. This phrase also characterises the tempter's voice – the hero's fault in flesh and blood – of Shakespearean tragedy. The temptation scenes are precisely that: a challenge to the 'ego personality'. And the correct reply, as we have seen, is to assert the integrity of the central self: 'I am nothing altered; what I was, I am.'

Shakespeare's use of dual figures is, then, not arbitrary; for it appears to touch the bedrock of psychology. The imagination naturally projects the archetypes on to individuals, creating dual figures unconsciously. Shakespeare does so deliberately; because he has learnt the art, as distinct from the science, of psychoanalysis from medieval poetry. The science of it belongs to the twentieth century; the art was in full flower in the thirteenth. And by this I mean that a psychoanalytical technique was then being used for artistic creation as consciously as a psychiatrist uses one to-day for the healing of a neurosis; and these two objectives, the creative and the curative, are curiously akin; indeed, in Shakespeare's resolutions of tragedy, they are almost the same. The principles of allegorical construction which stem from the *Roman de la Rose*, Shakespeare applies to the healing of the tragic wound.

It is characteristic of a poet that he should have more easy access to the unconscious than the majority, and the greater the poet, the fuller his exploration is likely to be. This is true of Virgil, who was looked on as a magician in the Middle Ages; and it is true of Dante. Shakespeare's personifications of Love, the allegorical aspect of Dante's Beatrice, and the Anima of psychoanalysis, are certainly akin. However different they appear, they have an archetypal identity. Beatrice, more obviously than Shakespeare's heroines, is dual: she is the girl Dante saw on the bridge, the woman who distracted him in church, and probably an ordinary young Florentine; but when the projection of Dante's Anima is added to her, she is transformed into the guide of his soul, leading him to paradise, of whom he exclaims:

*O, isplendor di viva luce eterna!**

The fusion of the individual and the archetypal, the real and the allegorical, is almost as nearly perfect here as imagination can make it; but it is also wonderfully clearcut, for Dante is a conscious artist: for him, the real and the allegorical, the incarnate woman and the celestial guide, are two 'beauties', the one within the other; and the 'splendour of living and eternal light', is the second beauty:

* 'O, splendour of eternal, living light!' *Purgatorio* XXXI.

*La seconda bellezza che tu cele.**

This second beauty, hidden within, is, in Shakespeare's heroines, the Love that to reject is tragedy and to follow is redemption. When Hamlet kills Polonius and disavows Ophelia, when Angelo disregards Escalus and spurns Mariana, they are as much lost, allegorically, as Dante would have been had he wandered alone in the world of souls without Virgil or Beatrice. But however much Dante may regard Virgil and Beatrice as objective existences, they correspond to archetypal patterns in his own soul nevertheless; and it is these, projections out of the depths of himself, that are his true psychopomps. A neurotic patient is also a soul that is lost; and the work of the psychiatrist is not to become his guide, but to show him that there is a guiding power in himself. 'Since no outward support is of any use to them,' writes Jung, 'they must finally discover it in themselves – admittedly the most unlikely place from the rational point of view, but an altogether possible one from the point of view of the unconscious.'†

The analogies are so strong that it is reasonable to draw the inference that we are confronted here not by opinions, predilections or poetic invention, but by psychical facts. It is not just a charming notion on Shakespeare's part to assert, in allegory, that the symbol of love must not be cast out, or tragedy will ensue; there is an archetypal reality behind the symbol without which the soul really is lost. Much that has been expressed by the arts, in the centuries when they were the prime activity of genius, is now being confirmed by science in another language.

---

* 'The second beauty which you now conceal', *Purgatorio*, XXXI.
† *Psychology and Alchemy*, p.28.

Some of Blake's illustrations of the *Purgatorio* make the same statement in terms of visual art. His engraving of Beatrice leading Dante up the rocky path clearly suggests the peril of a soul that refuses the ideal guide. This conception of the path which can be mounted or descended – light above, darkness below and the pilgrim soul between – is wonderfully expressive of the principles of Shakespearean construction. The point is so important that I hope I may be pardoned for repetition: all Shakespeare's protagonists are envisaged by him as wayfarers on a similar steep road, at the bottom of which is the tragic act, chaos and death, while at the summit is creative mercy, cosmos and divine rebirth. The response to the temptations, which are the critical scenes, determine the direction of movement. The accepting of the guidance of Fidelity and Love – variously personified in each play – ensures the correct answer; but when these are rejected, there is always another guide – the ghost, the witches, Iago – personifying the sinister and retrograde contents of the psyche, ready to lead downwards to crime and disintegration. It is a choice between the Anima at her fairest and the Shadow at its worst. But both these guides, in their allegorical and psychoanalytical sense, are within: both of them affirm, as did Iago to Othello, 'I am thine own for ever.' 'If', says Jung, 'the Supreme Value and the Supreme Negation are outside, then the soul is void: its highest and its lowest are missing.' That the soul is never void, is, as we have seen, one of Shakespeare's cardinal principles.

15

The Tempest:
Tragic Pattern Reversed

I WILL NOT ATTEMPT a full discussion of *The Tempest*, partly from a sense of my incompetence and partly because it would introduce new problems and confuse the issue of our present quest. But in so far as *The Tempest* illustrates the points we have already raised, it forms a natural conclusion, and within these strict limits it must be examined.

In saying that *The Tempest* forms a natural conclusion, I do not mean that it is a satisfactory end to Shakespeare's work, or that he thought of it as such. Without a doubt, he had set himself the task of resolving his tragedies; and remarkable as the achieved resolutions are, the ascending souls have still not the tremendous power and conviction of those that fell.

Shakespeare died at the age of fifty-two, and so far from being written-out, he was then engaged in exploring another ocean. None of his successors in the theatre, except Goethe in *Faust*, has embarked upon it since. And Shakespeare's so-called retirement in his early forties was more like a setting-sail upon a voyage of discovery.

L'acqua ch'io prendo giammai non si corse:
*Minerva spira, e conducemi Apollo.**

The thought behind Dante's superb lines must have been matched in Shakespeare's mind when he began to work on his last plays; and if he had not died in early middle-age he might have created, and would almost certainly have tried to create, a regenerate hero of the stature of Macbeth. Prospero is not that hero; but rather, as it seems to me, a splendid promise of such a man. In Shakespeare's *Divine Comedy*, the *Paradise* is unfinished; but I do not doubt that it existed in his mind, and that he conceived the essence of it in harmony with Dante's final line:

l'Amor che muove il sole e l'altre stelle.†

Shakespeare's last plays are much more religious than they at first appear. The higher religions are all agreed that the proper outcome of life is not the endurance of suffering but its cessation: the Christian resurrection, the Buddhist enlightenment, the Taoist immortalisation, the perfection of yoga and the theophanies of classical drama all affirm the same victory. Shakespeare's plays of healing take up this traditional theme, which is, indeed, life's supreme challenge to practical philosophy.

When Shakespeare came to *The Tempest*, he was an adept at condensing the tragedy he was about to resolve. In *Measure for Measure*, the resolution proper is mainly confined to the last act, and in *The Winter's Tale*, to the last two; but in *The Tempest*, most of the play is given to it, and

* 'The seas I venture were never sailed before: Minerva blows and Apollo steers', *Paradiso*, II,7.
† 'The love that moves the sun and the other stars', *Paradiso*.

the tragedy is recapitulated in brief, deft strokes. If we are alert to Shakespeare's allegories, we find Antonio, the usurper and doer of the tragic act, characterised by the first words spoken to him. The boatswain, who is doing his utmost to save the ship, and is therefore part of the theme of resolution, says to him:

You mar our labour ... you assist the storm.

We have noticed elsewhere that Shakespearean storms are the counterparts of tragedy. Antonio, Alonso and Sebastian are a group of down-going souls in a quite literal sense; they sink, their ship dashed to pieces; but none of them is lost. The potential tragedy is being watched – as it was in *Measure for Measure* – by an all-directing mind. And we are to witness another demonstration of the redemption, by creative mercy, of souls that are morally guilty of the tragic crime.

In the second scene we are introduced to Prospero, and are at once among familiar themes. Prospero is a man of power; and he has earned it, by taking much the same steps as the Duke of Vienna, of which the first was the study and improvement of himself:

I pray thee, mark me.
I, thus neglecting worldly ends, all dedicated
To closeness and the bettering of my mind ...

Both of them, also, 'rapt in secret studies', placed too much confidence in other people. At a certain stage of progress this may be inevitable; but the resultant trouble cannot be ignored; it has to be suffered and cured. And the cure, as expounded in *The Tempest*, shows us the regeneration sequence set out completely as the tragic pattern reversed. As with Florizel, Prospero is displayed to us as a soul containing a principle of strength which will enable him to triumph when he is tested. His formed studies constitute a part of this strength, but by no means all of it. The greater secret lies in his relation to Miranda.

Whatever else Miranda may be – and perhaps she symbolises more than the heroines we have so far discussed – she is certainly, as they were, Love. Love in the allegorical or archetypal sense, not as an object, but as a quality in Prospero's own soul to which he must be faithful if the tragic sickness is to be healed. Hence the cardinal importance of his line:

I have done nothing but in care of thee.

That is his pillar of strength – he has conceived and cherished the quality of love within himself; none the less, he is far from being wholly regenerate: he has his Caliban.

This second scene is for Prospero a temptation; because his enemies are in his hands, and revenge is open to him. The island might have become another Elsinore. There is no outward circumstance to prevent this. He could have demanded justice – like Hamlet, Angelo, Isabella, Othello, Leontes – passed death-dooms, as they did, and moralised, as they did, with specious magnificence. Or he might simply have watched the course of 'poetic' justice, and seen his enemies plot, and finally murder one another. It is one of Shakespeare's fundamental propositions that tragedy begets tragedy, for ever and ever, until someone has the strength, the courage and the understanding to say, Enough!

Ethically, the most obvious significance of Prospero, in the long procession of Shakespearean heroes, is that he is sufficiently evolved to do this. Enough of death for death, wife for wife, cut for thrust! Enough of this ever-widening sea of blood, this ever-growing mountain of corpses! Let there be self-knowledge, love, creative mercy, regeneration, and man new made! And there will be, but not easily. In spite of Prospero's long preparation, this moment is still a test:

> By accident most strange, bountiful Fortune,
> Now my dear lady, hath mine enemies
> Brought to this shore; and by my prescience
> I find my zenith doth depend upon
> A most auspicious star, whose influence
> If now I court not, but omit, my fortunes
> Will ever after droop.

In other words, we stand at one of the predestined cross-roads to which Shakespeare always brings us. Everything now hangs upon the hero's decision, which is not forced upon him by outward circumstances, but is a moral action taken in his own soul. If he turns to the right, a conclusive victory is possible; if he turns to the left, everything may yet go wrong. At such moments in Shakespearean drama, fate seems to be waiting, like a huge machine, for the hero to put it into motion; it does not compel him – the controlling levers are in himself; but once he has manipulated them, the machine will begin to move, carrying him, with gathering momentum, to what appears, though falsely, to be a predetermined end.

> Go on, I'll follow thee!
> You shall not go, my Lord.
> Hold off your hands!
> Be rul'd; you shall not go.

These fate-deciding moments are in every play; and the reply of Hamlet, 'My fate cries out', is the wrong one. Those who make it are the spiritual underlings, and the fault is in themselves. An affirmation of self-sovereignty is the correct answer, 'To this I am most constant, though destiny say no.'

Prospero had made sufficient progress to be constant; and if Fortune is no longer a fickle mistress, but his bountiful lady, the cause is a change in himself and not in her. And Miranda, of course, is the principle of his power – more than his book, more than his knowledge or his magic staff; she guides him as unerringly as Beatrice guided Dante, and far more sweetly, for she is unconscious of her rôle. It is Miranda, who may be conceived as a whisper from the divine element in himself (somewhat as Bialacoil is the voice of the lady's gracious self), who helps him in this test. In everything she says, she is the ally and advocate of his own creative mercy:

> If by your art, my dearest father, you have
> Put the wild waters in this roar, allay them. ...
> O, I have suffer'd
> With those that I saw suffer! ...
> O, the cry did knock
> Against my very heart!
> Had I been any god of power, I would
> Have sunk the sea within the earth, or ere
> It should the good ship so have swallowed and
> The fraughting souls within her.

Even when he tells her the full story of Antonio's villainy – which was 'a brother's murder', and here we touch Hamlet again, but with a creative instead of a destructive reaction from the 'ghost' – Miranda comments:

O, the heavens!
Alack, for pity!

And when he speaks of Gonzalo – who is old Fidelity, invariably linked with Love – she exclaims:

>   Would I might
> But ever see that man!

By the middle of the second scene, then, Shakespeare has already outlined a pattern which, by following it in other plays, he has led us to expect. Antonio – with Alonso and Sebastian as his collaborators – is a down-going soul who has committed, morally, the tragic act, and so 'assists the storm'. Prospero is a mounting soul who has won a measure of self-knowledge, preserved Love, 'even to the edge of doom', and is successfully passing his first test. Miranda is the archetype of Love and Beauty, which the soul must always shelter. And Gonzalo – 'holy Gonzalo', he is later called, reminding us of priest-like Camillo – is Fidelity, whose counsel is integrity to Self and to Heaven.

It is to these two, Miranda and Gonzalo, Love and Fidelity, allegorically conceived as qualities within himself, that Prospero owes his salvation. And he has sufficient self-knowledge to be aware of this; for he says to Miranda:

>   O, a cherubim
> Thou wast that did preserve me. Thou didst smile,
> Infused with a fortitude from heaven ...

While in the last act, he says to Gonzalo:

>   O, good Gonzalo,
> My true preserver, and a loyal sir

To him thou follow'st! I will pay thy graces
Home both in word and deed.

Shakespeare is being consistent in the use of his double
figures; and in view of the evidence from psychoanalysis it
does not seem unreasonable to think that the most important of them embody archetypes of the unconscious mind.
If so, it should be noted that this method of construction,
which may strike us as artificial, is really close to psychological truth. And it is also relevant that the up-going and
down-going movement of souls is clearly represented in
the *Passion Play*, in which the Judas-sequence leads down
to tragedy, and the Christ sequence up to regeneration,
with temptation scenes figuring in each.

Although Prospero's enemies were brought to the
island by 'bountiful Fortune' and 'accident most strange',
the shipwreck itself was the work of his magic. And this
brings us to another similarity with the redemption
process we have seen in other plays – the confrontation
with death. When the downward movement of the soul is
to be checked, and then reversed, it seems to be part of
Shakespeare's technique to use shock-therapy to bring it
to a first halt. We have seen how the Duke of Vienna used
this method of 'making heavenly comforts of despair' on
all the people he set right: each of them was faced with
death, either his own or that of someone he loved, as a preliminary to a fuller realisation of life. This treatment was
also administered to Leontes: the death of his son brought
his downward career to a stop. And now we find Prospero,
by arranging a most terrifying shipwreck, doing the same
thing. Everyone on board is faced with death, which is
shown as a turning-point in life; so that Gonzalo exclaims,

not without a touch of dry humour in spite of the dreadful situation:

> The king and prince at prayers! Let's assist them,
> For our case is theirs.

The second remark is no doubt intended to include the audience; and this regular Shakespearean usage is probably another debt to the medieval theatre. We need look no further than *Everyman*, which had its first printing about 1520, for the most likely proximate source. God sends Death to give Everyman a shock, the consequence of which is that Everyman puts his life in order (in the conventional theological sense) and makes a good end. When we see that Shakespeare often uses the *idea* of death for a similar purpose in his own regeneration pattern, it is reasonable to think that he may be indebted to the crude old allegory, but has refined it with great skill.

If this is so, it is an illuminating example of the way in which Shakespeare transforms what he borrows; and to compare the naïvety of the suggestion with the subtlety of the development is yet another measure of his greatness. Resemblance, of course, is no proof of derivation; and a single instance would be nothing worth. But Shakespeare seems to have taken many ideas from the old theatre, and to have sublimated them so finely that their origins are all but lost. When however, we notice repetitions in his pattern, in play after play, then we are compelled to look for precedents.

To return to Prospero, the opening of *The Tempest* is a test of his constancy. As the Duke of Vienna observed, 'it is virtuous to be constant in any undertaking', but it is not easy; and without the help of Miranda – which is not merely her influence at a critical moment but the consequence of cherishing her through the preceding years – Prospero would have failed. Had he treated her as Leontes or Lear behaved to their daughters, his fortunes would certainly have drooped. In the world of Shakespearean allegory, that would have been a simple matter of cause and effect; and so it is hardly possible to over-stress the inner significance of the line:

> O, a cherubim
Thou wast that did preserve me.

When Prospero has passed his first test, we should expect, as with Florizel, a counterpart to the tragic inner conflict in the form of a confirmatory experience of increasing sovereignty of soul. We get it emphatically; but not in the form of a soliloquy. Prospero's advance towards a consolidation of the inner kingdom is staged for us in an allegorical action. Directly after the test, Ariel and Caliban are introduced.

There can be no doubt that Ariel and Caliban – irrespective of what they may signify in their own right – are both incarnate contents of Prospero's soul. In dealing with them, he is dealing with aspects of himself; and that is the most important, subtle and difficult transaction that every man who is striving for self-realisation has to undertake. We will consider the allegory of Ariel and Caliban later; meanwhile, it is evident that the willing service of the higher, and obedience of the lower natures are prerequisites of a spiritual advance. Provisionally, we may see these two as divine service born of love, and inferior service made under compulsion; and these are the first characteristics of Ariel and Caliban that Shakespeare makes explicit. The one is displayed in Ariel's greeting to Prospero:

> All hail, great master! grave sir, hail! I come
> To answer thy best pleasure; be't to fly,
> To swim, to dive in the fire, to ride
> On the curl'd clouds, to thy strong bidding task
> Ariel and all his quality.

The second theme, to be enlarged later, is touched on in Prospero's words:

> We'll visit Caliban my slave ...
>   ... he does make our fire,
> Fetch in our wood, and serves in offices
> That profit us. What, ho! slave! Caliban!
> Thou earth, thou! speak.

These are confirmatory signs greater than they at first appear. But it is not Shakespeare's intention to show Prospero as a perfect man; if he were, tests and temptations would have ceased to have meaning for him, and so serve neither an ethical nor a dramatic purpose. Prospero still has passions to fight; and there is still some power in them, and some concession to them also. When his second test comes at the close of Act IV some condign punishment is meted out:

> Let them be hunted soundly. At this hour
> Lie at my mercy all mine enemies.

From Shakespeare's ideal point of view, according to which power divine should be paramount, there is a strong touch of unregeneracy in that! But Prospero's constancy is of a high order, and he has moved so far along the up-going path, by his own efforts, that there is no incarnate tempter to pour poison in his ear. Shakespeare's reversal of the tragic sequence is complete in all respects; so that the tempter's voice is replaced by what might be called a whisper from heaven. In the first test, as we saw, this came from Miranda. In the second, it comes from Ariel:

> Your charm so strongly works 'em,
> That if you now beheld them, your affections
> Would become tender.

Prospero responds to this, and comes out of his second test as triumphantly as Florizel; he exclaims:

> Though with their high wrongs I am struck to the quick,
> Yet with my nobler reason 'gainst my fury
> Do I take part: the rarer action is
> In virtue than in vengeance: they being penitent,
> The sole drift of my purpose doth extend
> Not a frown further. Go, release them ...

This is victory. And immediately after we have a soliloquy, reaching towards a higher plane of spiritual sovereignty, beyond 'rough magic'. Then music sounds – music with the power to comfort and to cure. It is no longer Prospero who needs the consolation and the healing, but his enemies: in other words, creative mercy is now to be made manifest as a transforming power:

> The charm dissolves apace;
> And as the morning steals upon the night,
> Melting the darkness, so their rising senses
> Begin to chase the ignorant fumes that mantle
> Their clearer reason.

The act of creative mercy, which corresponds to the tragic act, is then proclaimed:

You, brother mine …
              … I do forgive thee,
Unnatural though thou art.

In place of the realisation of horror, we are shown the dawning of a rational, and ultimately a celestial light and understanding:

              Their understanding
Begins to swell; and the approaching tide
Will shortly fill the reasonable shore
That now lie foul and muddy.

Prospero, like the Duke of Vienna, is exhibiting the power of forth-going virtue; and Alonso, at least, is aware of this, for he says:

            … since I saw thee,
The affliction of my mind amends, with which,
I fear, a madness held me.

And it is to be noticed that Shakespeare links crime with ignorance, and that his resolutions of tragedy all contain a promise of full explanation and understanding. The words of the Duke of Vienna would be appropriate to any of them:

Look, the unfolding star calls up the shepherd. Put not yourself into amazement how these things should be: all difficulties are but easy when they are known.

And Prospero concludes with the promise:

        I'll deliver all.

The ninth phase of Shakespeare's regeneration sequence, matching death in the tragedies, is the symbolic union of love. There are several love-unions at the end of

Measure for Measure, two in *The Winter's Tale* and one in *The Tempest*. The allegorical significance might be cryptically expressed by the text, God is love. In Shakespeare's allegories it implies that the hero who has reached self-knowledge realises that the Self is essentially divine and at one with love; and from this comes the second or spiritual birth; for 'God is love' in the sense that a higher power, or transcendent function, unites the jarring opposites in harmony, which is 'man new made'.

There is even an alchemical counterpart to this – of which Shakespeare was probably aware, since the philosophy lying behind alchemy was much studied in his time – in the *conjunctio* of Sol and Luna, which marks the completion of the alchemical work. In fact, the theme of a Sacred Marriage, in one form or another, is so wellnigh universal that it is doubtless a sacrament in the sense that it points to some inner experience arising spontaneously under appropriate conditions.

The union of love which closes the plays of regeneration is something other than the happy ending of a comedy, although they are related. Shakespeare is drawing on the tradition of the mystical marriage, perhaps with special relation to the medieval religion of love; but the ultimate origin of such similitudes is to be looked for in the structure of the psyche, and not in the many allegories of religion, myth and doctrine which are projections into consciousness of an inner event the real nature of which is unknown. To Shakespeare, love and beauty are, as the unconscious reveals them, virtually interchangeable; the deity of the one is the deity of the other; they are the dynamic and static aspects of the same thing: love is beauty in action, and beauty is love at rest.

I do not propose to broach the further problems of *The Tempest*; but a few words on Ariel and Caliban may help to support the view that in his relations with them Prospero is dealing with himself. If these two figures are not allegorical, then they are moonbeams; and I am convinced that Shakespeare, at this point in his career, believed that he had something of more importance to set down.

'This thing of darkness I acknowledge mine,' says Prospero of Caliban. And when Caliban is introduced, his first answer, as the stage directions tell us, is from 'within'. It is never a kind answer. In other words, Caliban symbolises the unregenerate elements in Prospero himself. Every soul possesses such a brutish and still intractible residue of former darkness, and it has to be dealt with; in genuine analysis, it cannot be disowned. Neither Prospero nor anyone else enjoys the task of educating his Caliban; but it is an unavoidable labour that must be continued, though seldom patiently, until the base element is refined.

Unless the brute is tamed, by a mixture of severity and kindness, it lurks as a potential traitor, awaiting its chance for murder and usurpation, in the citadel of the soul. The majority of Shakespeare's plays illustrate this idea, and Caliban is an incarnation of it. He would have raped Miranda, had he been able; which is yet another symbol of the debasement of love that the tragic protagonists all allow to happen in themselves. He mistook liquor for the wine of life; and this consequent intoxication is a base form of the tragic madness. Finally, he would have murdered Prospero, and so brought to pass the ninth phase of tragedy – the hero's death.

Caliban is one more embodiment of the soul's Shadow, and the innermost cause, when it is permitted to be, of the hero's downfall. Prospero differs from the doomed ones because he has knowledge of both the dark and light side of himself. But Caliban is redeemable, and at the end he says:

> I'll be wise hereafter,
> And seek for grace.

When this happens, and the 'thing of darkness' has been changed to light, Prospero himself will be a power divine; and therefore he continues with the education of the monster, although it is an uncongenial task. It is for this reason that Prospero's ability, first to compel obedience, and then to instil some light into Caliban, are confirmatory signs of an increasing lordship of the soul.

Ariel is the most difficult as he is the most delicate allegorical problem; but he is clearly too important to be left out. I approach him with diffidence. He must not escape the net altogether, and yet it would be wrong to entangle him too far. I will therefore offer my suggestions, but make no claims. His chief characteristics are that he does Prospero's bidding, but he longs and has the right to be set free. His service is contrasted with that of Caliban; and it may be that it signifies the divine service that is, or should be, perfect freedom. That would not be out of keeping with his past; for in the days of the foul witch Sycorax, the service of love was allowed no expression at all, but was imprisoned in the smitten tree of life.

If that is a part of Ariel's meaning, then further light may be shed on it by Gonzalo's speech, in the first scene of the second act, on his ideal state. Everyone in his commonwealth, says Gonzalo, shall be idle, and it will be like the golden age. But the paradox of perfect idleness is that it is also perfect activity. And if Shakespeare had been looking for an illustration of this, he could scarcely have found one better than joy beneath the blossom on the bough.

That service and freedom and joy are among his qualities is too vague a finding to be of critical use, but I fear the futility of trying to tie Ariel down. Still, I hold to the view that as an allegorical figure he is a part of Prospero; and so his liberation may be intended to suggest that the service Prospero will give to others in future will not be a duty exacted, but a free act of joy. Prospero is on the path of perfection, and nothing less would be fitting for a divine man.

16

The Pattern for Regeneration

SHAKESPEARE would appear to have worked out a dramatic pattern of regeneration which exactly balanced the tragic sequence. It is the same road travelled in the opposite direction, and the corresponding phases may now be summarised.

FIRST: We are shown a soul containing the principles of strength which will enable it to pass the coming tests.

SECOND: The voice or voices of the higher Self, which will help the hero in his temptations, are characterised for us.

THIRD: There is a test or temptation scene, in which the hero triumphs, because he is true to the Self and faithful to Love.

FOURTH: There is a confirmatory experience, tending towards inner sovereignty or lordship of the soul.

FIFTH and SIXTH: There is a second test, and a second confirmation.

SEVENTH: The act of creative mercy, including self-forgiveness.

EIGHTH: An experience of enlightenment.

NINTH: The symbolic union of love.

We have already suggested that the two contrasting patterns are probably related to the Christ-sequence and the Judas-sequence, and were therefore derived from the old religious drama; and this is likely to be true also of the confrontation with death, a form of shock-therapy which Shakespeare regularly administers to the soul about to change from the downward movement to the upward. Trials according to the old law, which Shakespeare repudiates, and in which the just is frequently condemned by the unjust, may be of similar origin.

The first condition, many times reiterated, of entering the path of ascent is, 'to thine own self be true'. And Shakespeare makes it abundantly clear in successive plays that a spiritual interpretation of the Self is here intended. The little conscious self of everyday life makes no sense at all in this regenerative context. However he arrived at this conception, which is theologically heretical, Shakespeare is in harmony here with the Perennial Philosophy. Describing the fundamentals of this, Aldous Huxley says:

> Man possesses a double nature, a phenomenal ego and an eternal Self, which is the inner man, the spirit, the spark of divinity within the soul. It is possible for a man, if he so desires, to identify himself with the spirit and therefore with the Divine Ground, which is of the same or like nature with the spirit.*

It would be difficult to put more succinctly what Shakespeare implies by truth to one's self and integrity to heaven. Linked with this, in Shakespeare's allegorical pattern, is fidelity to love; and we can tell immediately

---

* *Bhagavad-Gita*, translation Prabhavananda and Isherwood, introducdon by Aldous Huxley.

whether, in his intention, the hero is moving up or down by his relation to the allegorical figure representing love.

We must also bear in mind that Shakespeare's deepest thought is always close to the spirit of the Gospels. In the introduction to *Psychology and Alchemy*, Jung shows that Christ is one of several symbols of the archetype of the Self; but he adds later,* 'This tremendous conclusion failed to dawn on the medieval mind.' However – perhaps with the help of St Paul, 'Christ liveth in me' – it may well have dawned on Shakespeare; and it is, in any case, implicit in his ethical argument. It is the essential principle for the establishment of harmony between the Christian and the Perennial Philosophy, and by revealing the Supreme Value within each soul, it completely validates Shakespeare's moral standard, 'To thine own self be true.' The final link between the tragic hero, who betrays his own Self, and Judas, who betrays Christ, is thus forged.

Turning to the ascending path, we may now see why those characters who symbolise the higher self – which is the relation, for example, of the Duke of Vienna to Angelo – must be engaged upon a Christ-like task and exhibit 'power divine'. In the last act the duke is shown as, at the same time, both judge and saviour. This, of course, is the symbolic role of Christ; and the full meaning of Shakespearean justice now becomes clear. We have already seen that, in Shakespeare's view, justice without love becomes tyranny; we may now go further, and say that the function of true justice is salvation. The proposition is established again in Prospero; and also, in the ultimate spiritual sense, in Leontes, who exemplifies self-judgment at the end

* I p.341.

of the third act, and self-forgiveness at the opening of the fifth: in the last analysis, then, the Supreme Value, the Judge-Saviour of every soul, is its own true Self, which is a spiritual or supra-personal principle.

Seen against this background, Shakespearean trial scenes, like the temptations, are invested with an unsuspected importance. As in the *Passion Play*, it is really the judges and the law that are on trial; and by the sentence they pass on the accused they are themselves condemned. But there is also a higher justice, and of that we may affirm, because it is inseparable from love, that its function, whether in the world or in the soul, is salvation. The contrasting of these two standards of justice is one of the most frequent and important themes in Shakespeare. It appears early and continues to the end of his work. The justice of the bond, which Shylock demanded, is that of the old law; the justice he received, from the Duke of Venice, is that of the new:

> That thou shalt see the difference of our spirit,
> I pardon thee thy life before thou ask it.

Pardon, indeed, is the word to all

Appendix – *Titus Andronicus*

SOME SEVENTEEN YEARS before he wrote *The Tempest*, Shakespeare had begun to sup full with horrors in *Titus Andronicus*. And a backward glance at this snakepit, from the subtleties of Prospero's isle, indicates, though it cannot measure, the immensity of his journey. There is one other thing that a consideration of these extremes will show – Shakespeare's fidelity to his own principles. He was no weather-cock in his ethics; he took advantage of the changing fashions of the stage, but always as a master; he must have had a measure, perhaps an over-full measure, of human frailty; but his ideal stood:

I will be true, despite thy scythe and thee.

To appreciate this continuity, let us now turn back almost twenty years.

The most probable theory of the authorship* of *Titus Andronicus* is that the original play was written by Peele, and that it was revised and expanded, early in 1594, by Peele and Shakespeare in collaboration. This furbishing was done in haste, probably to meet an advertised date of production; and Peele seems to have revised the first act, and Shakespeare the rest.

In the matter of polishing lines and speeches, they could have worked independently. But they must have consulted

* See Dover Wilson's Introduction, *Titus Androntcus*, Cambridge edition.

together on questions affecting the plot. And since Shakespeare's imaginative and intellectual ability was so incomparably the greater, and since the play afterwards bore his name, it is fair to suppose that alterations to the plot-structure, by whichever partner they were carried out, were of his inspiration. It is therfore interesting to notice that the additions to the original which can be detected tend to bring the play into line with the constructional principles that we have found in Shakespeare's own. If the revision was done as Dover Wilson suggests, in about a fortnight, it would have been impossible for Shakespeare to have reshaped the play altogether; but what he appears to have given it, apart from burnishing the poetry, is a trace of his system.

In the opening scene there are three insertions into the original play. They were probably written by Peele; but, I submit, at Shakespeare's suggestion; because, besides the general reasons already stated, the episodes they add are of the kind that Shakespeare would have naturally put in, if he had been re-casting the play in conformity with his own theories. Let us first take a look at the context.

Peele's initial situation shows us two candidates, one bad and the other good, both seeking to be elected emperor of Rome. They address their supporters. Saturninus says:

Plead my successive title with your swords.

And Bassianus:

Let desert in pure election shine ...

The audience is in no doubt as to which would be the better emperor; but someone has to make the momentous choice. Titus Andronicus, an old general returning with captives and spoils from a successful war against the Goths, is authorised to decide. This is not presented as a Shakespearean test of his morals, but merely of his judgment.

We are then told more about Titus. His background is not unlike that of Macbeth. He is a man of whom the world holds a golden opinion, but he is a man of blood. And because he is a man of blood – like David, who could not for that reason build the temple – he is certain, according to Shakespearean logic, to choose wrong. He does so; and Saturninus is elected. But before this happens, we come to the first interpolation.

Lines 96 to 149 have been inserted. Titus had twenty-five sons; all but four have been killed in battle, and a sacrifice is to be made to their ghosts. The inserted lines describe this sacrifice. The victim is Alarbus, eldest son of Tamora, the captive queen of the Goths. We will consider why Shakespeare, as I suppose, suggested this scene in a moment.

In the second interpolation, Titus kills one of his own sons, Mutius. The reason for this is that Mutius stands up for his sister, Lavinia. Titus not only makes the mistake of choosing the wrong emperor, but follows it up by giving him Lavinia in marriage. Lavinia, however, is betrothed to Bassianus; Bassianus claims her, and they escape. Mutius prevents his father from following them, and in consequence he is killed. Dover Wilson says, 'Mutius, indeed, is a quite unnecessary complication, and I suggest that his death at the hands of Titus has also been added. But I have no wish to stress this last point.' The point, however, needs to be established if any deductions are to be made from it; and I will therefore attempt to do so.

Titus says to Saturninus in line 289:

Follow, my lord, and I'll soon bring her back.

In line 299, Saturninus says:

No, Titus, no, the emperor needs her not.

To omit the intervening ten lines – in the course of which Mutius is killed – makes for smoother reading, which suggests that the episode has been added.

In the next forty lines there is no mention of the dead Mutius. Saturninus proposes marriage to Tamora; and Titus seems to have nothing on his mind except that he is not invited to the wedding. In line 338, he is complaining:

I am not bid to wait upon this bride.
Titus, when wert thou wont to walk alone,
Dishonoured thus and challenged of wrongs?

Then come fifty lines of argument as to whether Mutius is to be buried in the family tomb or not, till, in line 391, we are abruptly returned to the not-having-been-invited-to-the-wedding mood. And Marcus says:

My lord, to step out of these dreary dumps,
How comes it that the subtle Queen of Goths
Is of a sudden thus advanced in Rome?

The emotional continuity would of itself suggest that the burial scene had been interpolated, and there can be no doubt that Dover Wilson is right: the death of Mutius, and everything appertaining to it, has been added to the original plot.

Two deaths, then, have been put in. Titus is responsible for both. One is Tamora's son, and the other his own. Peele, apparently, wrote these scenes; but the over-all planning of the reconstruction of the play was, I feel sure, Shakespeare's. Why should he add two deaths? There is ample evidence that Shakespeare was personally revolted by blood; when he smears his scenes with it, it is not in pleasure but in protest. And certainly no play ever stood less in need of superfluous death than *Titus Andronicus*; even by the standards of the groundlings there was a glut of it, and I cannot believe that Shakespeare was privately amused by their bloody-mindedness; he shows too plainly elsewhere that it disgusted him. If two deaths were added at Shakespeare's suggestion, it can only have been for constructional or allegorical reasons. Let us, then, examine the inserted episodes in the light of Shakespeare's theory and practice in work that was entirely his own.

The first thing that we notice about the sacrifice of Alarbus is that it has the potentialities of a true Shakespearean temptation scene. They are not developed, because Peele wrote the scene; but if Shakespeare had written it from the basic idea, Titus could have been torn by opposing forces in his soul, as all Shakespearean tragic heroes are. This is because he is being compelled, in the typically Shakespearean manner, to make a moral decision. I will have mercy and not sacrifice; and it is between these that Titus must choose. His surviving sons claim a sacrifice for their brothers who have been killed. Lucius says:

> Give us the proudest prisoner of the Goths,
> That we may hew his limbs, and on a pile
> 'Ad manes fratrum' sacrifice his flesh ...

Titus gives them Tamora's eldest son. At this, she speaks:

Stay, Roman brethren! Gracious conqueror,
Victorious Titus, rue the tears I shed,
A mother's tears in passion for her son:
And if thy sons were ever dear to thee,
O, think my son to be as dear to me!

Measure for Measure lies ten years ahead, yet we cannot help thinking of the pleading of Isabella:

> Go to your bosom;
> Knock there, and ask your heart what it doth know ...

The argument is the same: put yourself in the victim's place, and then mercy will seem natural. The concluding lines of Tamora's speech have often been attributed to Shakespeare, on account of their thought-content, although the writing is probably Peele's:

Andronicus, stain not thy tomb with blood.
Wilt thou draw near the nature of the gods?
Draw near them then in being merciful:
Sweet mercy is nobility's true badge;
Thrice-noble Titus, spare my first-born son.

Again, it is Isabella's pleading, even more than Portia's, that is brought to mind. There are, of course, non-Shakespearean parallels as well; but these seem insignificant when we reflect that Shakespeare revised this play, and that the theme of creative mercy was, or was to become, his cardinal principle in the resolution of tragedy. Surely it must have been introduced here on his advice; for it carries with it the implication, essentially Shakespearean, that if Titus had shown mercy, the worst of the tragedy would have been averted. Peele was incapable of portraying an inner conflict in Titus as Shakespeare might have done; but the conception of the scene is such that a crisis of conscience, expressed in soliloquy, could have flowed from it.

Let us now compare this moral decision and its consequences with the other decision Titus had to make – purely Peele – in choosing an emperor. It offers no scope whatever for a conflict in the soul. Titus simply commits an Aristotelean 'error', from which calamity follows out of all proportion to the fault. This illuminates the contrast between the Aristotelean and the Shakespearean pattern. Behind the Aristotelean error, which precipitates tragedy, lies chance or fate: the yielding to temptation, whence a Shakespearean tragedy flows, is a moral decision. It is a principle with Shakespeare that the spirit is superior to fate. The fault is not in our stars, but in ourselves. Like Oedipus, Shakespeare's heroes come to a cross-roads; but if they kill their fathers there, they know what they're about; they soliloquise over it; and the audience understands why they afterwards tread the path to dusty death.

The interesting thing about Titus is that he does both. Peele's original play gives him an Aristotelean error; and Shakespeare, as I believe, interpolates a decision that was morally wrong. There is thus a dual origin of the sequent horrors. But whereas those that spring from the mere error seem nothing but 'motiveless malignity' on the part of Saturninus, those stemming from the sacrifice of Alarbus form a rational series. This clearly reveals the intellectual stiffening that Shakespeare gave to the play: he gave it, first of all, psychological motivation, which, illustrated by his habitual allegory, carries right through to the end.

Some of the sufferings of Titus are attributable to Saturninus; but, being unprovoked, they are neither ethically nor dramatically interesting. It is quite otherwise with the revenge sequence of which the fifty-one-line insertion of the sacrifice of Alarbus is the first term. Because Titus sacrifices Tamora's son, therefore she and her paramour successfully plot the death of two of his sons, therefore he kills and cooks two more of her sons, therefore Titus and Tamora both die. It is an *outré* example of Shakespeare's familiar proposition that revenge — including so-called justice — initiates an unending death-sequence, until an act of creative mercy lifts the curse.

The ideal of creative mercy is held up in the first insertion, and rejected. The ethical consequence of this rejection is enunciated by Marcus in the last act: it is a foreshadowing of the theme of *Hamlet* — race-suicide:

> Lest Rome herself be bane unto herself
> And she whom mighty kingdoms curts'y to,
> Like a forlorn and desperate castaway,
> Do shameful execution on herself.

This kind of plotting, which is really building a play upon an ethical theorem, is pure Shakespeare; and it would in itself be enough to show that he was the master-mind in the remodelling of the plot. But we find something more that is equally characteristic of him — an attempt to shore up the old fabric with an allegorical structure resembling his habitual design. It was not, of course, successful. The original was too recalcitrant, the revision was made at high speed, and once the play had been produced, Shakespeare had better things to do than to go on rewriting Peele. The interest does not lie in the achievement, but in the attempt; for it shows that even at this early date his highly individual principles of construction must have been shaped.

Let us first consider Shakespeare's retouching of Tamora. It would seem (from three lines that are found in the First Quarto, but nowhere else) that in Peele's version Titus had sacrificed an anonymous Goth before the opening. Shakespeare, as I presume, transformed the victim into Tamora's son, calling him:

> ... the noblest that survives,
> The eldest son of this distressed queen.

The change, as we have seen, gives motivation to her later conduct. Besides this, it is symbolic. When Alarbus is dead, nobility in Tamora is also dead. The Shakespearean inversion then ensues. The light side of her nature being gone, she turns to the dark side, which is symbolised by Aaron the Moor. She herself becomes the embodiment of Revenge, her remaining sons represent Murder and Rape, and later in the play they are all dressed up for these parts. In his mature work, Shakespeare would have been more subtle; there would have been no fancy clothes; but he would have maintained the meaning of the allegory. The fact that he is being crude in this case is a guide to his intentions when they are less clear. Although the allegory here lacks refinement, it is neatly balanced: the noble son, killed in the first act, is replaced by the black baby, in the fourth, the fruit of her union with Aaron.

In Peele's first version, it seems certain, there never was any nobility in Tamora. The penultimate line of the play, 'Her life was beastly', is his estimate of her, a static character without development, and therefore – whether beastly or goodly – dull. Shakespeare has done something to change this. Her first line, a part of the first interpolation, begins:

Stay, Roman brethren!

If this had been in the original, it would have been without significance. But it is the opening of the mercy speech, and the immediate context is the appeal – Think of my son as if he were your own son. This is essentially Shakespeare's human viewpoint, the brotherhood of man; and I therefore assume that 'Roman brethren' is intended to be sincere. If it is only rhetoric, then the themes of mercy and of doing-as-you-would-be-done-by are no better. But this is not so; because they are principles of Shakespeare's ethic, and he returns to them at the end of the play in the speech about Rome doing 'execution on herself'.

In the mercy-speech, then, Shakespeare has introduced a brief glimpse of something that never occurred to Peele – a noble, or potentially noble Tamora, who might have become a Roman 'adopted happily'. But Titus's act of 'cruel, irreligious piety' results in her being incorporated with Rome not as a daughter but as a fury. Even after she is a fury, Shakespeare still gives her, in the second act, some lovely lines:

And curtained with a counsel-keeping cave,
We may, each wreathed in the other's arms,
Our pastimes done, possess a golden slumber.

Clearly there can be no question of allegorical consistency in such a hotch-potch of a play; but we can discern, none the less, Shakespeare's characteristic touch. So it is with Aaron. Peele's Aaron must have been a mere villain:

Shakespeare has done something towards making him the dark side of Tamora's soul. He has no special motive of his own to be revenged on Titus; but he is the mind of her revenge. He not only plots it for her, but he holds her to this single, deadly purpose, even when her inclination is to love, and her thoughts stray to 'golden slumber' and 'sweet melodious birds'. He replies:

> Madam, though Venus govern your desires,
> Saturn is dominator over mine:
> What signifies my deadly-standing eye,
> My silence and my cloudy melancholy,
> My fleece of woolly hair that now uncurls
> Even as an adder when she doth unroll
> To do some fatal execution?
> No, madam, these are no venereal signs:
> Vengeance is in my heart, death in my hand,
> Blood and revenge are hammering in my head

Why? Peele would have been satisfied with unmotivated villainy; but he did not write that speech. Shakespeare's characters are never without motive – his own instinct for psychology and drama is too keen. It is Tamora's Shadow that is speaking here. And as Bialacoil was imprisoned by Daungere, and the lover expelled from the garden, so it is with her. And behind the whole of her revenge, pulling the wires – already a hint of an *éminence grise* – is the intelligence of Aaron.

There are equally suggestive additions to Peele's Lavinia. As a consistent love-symbol, she is past prayer; but there are moments when Shakespeare tries to see her, and indeed uses her, as such. This brings us to the second insertion – lines 289 to 299 – in which Titus kills one of his own sons. Before this, Titus had committed the error of giving Lavinia to the wrong husband; but in the inserted lines he is guilty of tragic crime: in his determination to drag Lavinia from her true lover, he yields to the temptation of killing his son. The contrast between an Aristotelean error and a Shakespearean sin for which the hero is morally responsible is exactly what we noticed before between the old context and the first insertion — between the error of choosing the wrong emperor and the guilt of sacrificing Tamora's son.

The conclusion seems inescapable, that the second insertion, like the first, was put in at Shakespeare's suggestion, even if Peele wrote it; and that, like the sacrifice, it constitutes the first term of another series of Shakespearean ideas. When we are accustomed to Shakespeare's allegorical patterns in other plays, his primary aim in inserting this episode is clear. For a moment, he is seeing Lavinia as his symbol of love. Titus does violence to love, and therefore he brings on tragedy. The fact that he kills his son puts him in line with all Shakespeare's tragic heroes: every one of them, allegorically speaking, kills the highest qualities in his own soul; in the moral sense, he destroys himself.

Lavinia is really beyond the pale as a love-symbol, and cannot be sustained as such for long. Her mutilated condition reflects the mutilated ideal of love in her father; but Shakespeare never took her to his heart. Nevertheless, he gives her some characterizing lines, as, for example, after her husband's murder:

For 'tis not life that I have begged so long,
Poor I was slain when Bassianus died.

Later in the play, he clearly admits her to be hopeless; though I find it hard to believe, with Dover Wilson, that he could have been so unkind as to burlesque her! The theme of Love cast out, degraded and murdered, always a concomitant of the tragic act, is one that haunts him. Still, it must be confessed that the image of Lavinia as a 'conduit with three issuing spouts' is more than most readers can take with a straight face. On the other hand, even sixteen years later, in a play written at leisure, and in a context where he was certainly not being funny, Shakespeare could say of Hermione that, 'gasping to begin some speech, her eyes became two spouts'. So may not poor mutilated Lavinia, under all the circumstances of relative inexperience and haste, be allowed, without mockery, one spout more?

The whole of this scene – Act II, Scene iv – may be an addition by Shakespeare to the original. And Dover Wilson virtually challenges the reader to 'conceive of Shakespeare writing such stuff in earnest at any period of his poetic development'. It is not beyond my own credulity. Goethe's tears for Werther were all sincere. And Wordsworth is deeply serious in his *Anecdote for Fathers*, showing how the practice of lying may be taught:

'Now, little Edward, say why so;
My little Edward, tell me why.'
'I cannot tell, I do not know.'
'Why, this is strange,' said I.

At this my boy hung down his head,
He blushed for shame, nor made reply;
And five times to the child I said,
'Why, Edward, tell me why?'

Surely, the works of great men all remind us what blush-making drivel the best of them can publish at his worst! I am forced to doubt that Shakespeare was laughing in this scene, because it is founded on ideas that he believed to be of sovereign importance. First, that the maltreatment of love leads to tragedy; and later, the converse, that the cherishing of love and beauty are linked with life itself:

> O, had the monster seen those lily hands
> Tremble like aspen leaves upon a lute,
> And make the silken strings delight to kiss them,
> He would not then have touched them for his life.
> Or, had he heard the heavenly harmony
> Which that sweet tongue hath made,
> He would have dropped his knife ...

Inspiration may not match intention, but Shakespeare means what he says here; because he goes on saying through the rest of his work that love, and nothing else, makes heavenly harmony. Lavinia, however inadequate, is for the moment his life-enhancing symbol of love. And I cannot think that he would mock the symbol, because he felt for it as Prospero did:

> I have done nothing but in care of thee.

Marcus, the brother of Titus, is the comforter of Lavinia in this scene. And he is, perhaps, a tentative sketch for the long line of portraits of old Fidelity, who is always connected with love. Even in the first act, though basically Peele, Marcus may have been retouched; and his first advice to Titus is that he should himself become emperor, which is perhaps to symbolise self-sovereignty:

Be 'candidatus' then ...
And help to set a head on headless Rome.

Titus refuses. Then, when Bassianus claims Lavinia as his bride, Marcus comes out boldly in their support:

This prince in justice seizeth but his own.

Titus calls him traitor, and immediately after kills his own son. In the next insertion, Marcus pleads for the burial of Mutius:

Suffer thy brother Marcus to inter
His noble nephew here in virtue's nest,
That died in honour and Lavinia's cause.
Thou art a Roman, be not barbarous ...

He is giving the right advice each time, and whenever Titus disregards it, trouble follows. In the second act we find Marcus as Lavinia's faithful comforter after her mutilation:

Do not draw back, for we will mourn with thee:
O, could our mourning ease thy misery!

In the last act it is he who warns Rome that she is doing 'shameful execution on herself', and adds:

But if my frosty signs and chaps of age,
Grave witnesses to true experience,
Cannot induce you to attend my words ...

All this is very like a sketch of the coming figures of Fidelity. He is a giver of good counsel on most, though not all occasions; and I take him to be a forerunner of a line that continues right through Shakespeare's work to old Gonzalo in *The Tempest*.

Many critics find little of interest in *Titus Andronicus*, and some would like to relieve Shakespeare of the responsibility of having had a hand in it. But it has something of the fascination of a ramshackle curiosity shop, in which surprising treasure lies among the cracked china and the spiders' webs. There are other pieces of this sort, odd jottings of themes that are expanded in other work; but only one more needs present mention. In the third addition to the first act – lines 341 to 390 – when Titus refuses to bury the son he has killed, Martius says:

He is not with himself ...

This is a Shakespearean note, indeed; and if Shakespeare did not write these insertions, then he wrote out of them for the rest of his life. It is unthinkable that he owed so much to Peele. However disjointed the play may be, it has clear traces, stemming from the additions to the first act, of his principles of construction. Nor do I think he found anything ludicrous in this abyss of horror. The character of Aaron is seriously drawn, and marks the lowest circle of the Shakespearean inferno. It may even owe something to the Satan of the religious drama, but subjectified. In his last speech, Aaron says:

If one good deed in all my life I did,
I do repent it from my very soul.

Shakespeare, like Dante, and some others among the very great, may have felt psychologically compelled to make the descent into hell. Aaron is the first of its many voices which could not be silenced:

And if it please thee! why, assure thee, Lucius,
'Twill vex thy soul to hear what I shall speak;
For I must talk of murders, rapes and massacres,
Acts of black night, abominable deeds,
Complots of mischief, treason, villainies
Ruthful to hear, yet piteously performed ...

For those six lines, we may forget Aaron. Shakespeare wrote them about the New Year of 1594, and he was surely looking into his own future. 'I *must* talk of these things!' And how thoroughly he did! Why? There is one good reason for visiting hell – to find and to show the way out. Descent may be, and perhaps must be, a preliminary to ascent; and from Shakespeare's hell there is an open but not an easy path to heaven. Essentially it is love's path. Truth to one's Self, fidelity to Love, and creative mercy are inseparable. This Shakespeare knew and said in *Titus Andronicus*. He was sure already that he knew the way, and that to reveal it was the chief purpose of his work. It is wrong to suppose that his final plays are the result of some kind of 'conversion'. They are the logical outcome of his life, a triumphant *Quod erat demonstrandum*.* In *Titus Andronicus*, using the voice of Marcus, he speaks to 'sad-faced men':

O! let me teach you how to knit again
This scatter'd corn into one mutual sheaf,
These broken limbs again into one body ...

That, as their ethical foundation shows, is what he is doing in his succeeding plays. He traces the soul's journey from the pit of chaos, to a point where it seems about to unfold celestial wings:

Mount, eagle, to my palace crystalline!

* (Q.E.D.), 'that has been proven'.

Author's Shakespearean References

(using *The Complete Works*, Oxford University Press)

53	And, in this upshot, purposes mistook	Ham 5.2.338
54	Man, proud man	MM 2.2.120
55	How would you be if He	MM 2.2.77
56	We have strict statutes and most biting laws	MM 1.3.19
57	... on whom it will, it will	MM 1.2.114
58	'Tis one thing to be tempted, Escalus	MM 2.1.17
59	Go to your bosom; Knock there, and ask your heart	MM 2.2.140
59	She speaks, and 'tis	MM 2.2.145
59	It is the law, not I condemn your brother	MM 2.2.82
59	Well, come to me to-morrow	MM 2.2.148
60	What's this? What's this?	MM 2.2.168
60	When I would pray and think	MM 2.4.1
60	O heavens!	MM 2.4.19
60	... redeem thy brother	MM 2.4.163
61	This deed unshapes me quite	MM 4.4.19
62	The, good prince	MM 5.1.367
63	And He that might the vantage best have took	MM 2.2.76
63	O, I will to him and pluck out his eyes!	MM 4.3.116
63	Thieves for their robbery have authority	MM 2.2.181
64	Be what you are, That is, a woman	MM 2.4.134
64	I dare do all that may become a man	Mac 1.7.46
64	... had he twenty heads to tender down	MM 2.4.180
66	... there my father's grave	MM 3.1.84
66	Sweet sister, let me live	MM 3.1.134
66	O, you beast!	MM 3.1.137
66	Take my defiance	MM 3.1.144
67	Mercy to thee would prove itself a bawd	MM 3.1.152
67	Not the king's crown, nor the deputed sword	MM 2.2.62
67	I would to heaven I had your potency	MM 2.2.69
69	Thyself and thy belongings	MM 1.1.29
69	Heaven doth with us as we with torches do	MM 1.1.33
70	If any in Vienna be of worth	MM 1.1.22
70	I hold you as a thing ensky'd and sainted	MM 1.4.33
71	Love you the man that wrong'd you?	MM 2.3.26
71	Yes; as I love the woman that wronged him	MM 2.3.27
72	Which sorrow is always towards ourselves	MM 2.3.34
72	I do repent me, as it is an evil	MM 2.3.37
72	There rest	MM 2.3.38
73	I humbly thank you	MM 3.1.42
73	Most ignorant of what he's most assured	MM 2.2.122

97	Within these three days let me hear thee say	Oth 3.3.475
97	My friend is dead	Oth 3.3.476
98	... and thou His cupbearer	WT 1.2.314
98	... mightst bespice a cup	WT 1.2.318
98	This is all	WT 1.2.348
98	I have trusted thee, Camillo	WT 1.2.237
99	Camillo, As you are certainly a gentleman	WT 1.2.390
99	I beseech you If you know aught	WT 1.2.394
99	Give me thy hand	WT 1.2.447
99	Be ruled; you shall not go	Ham 1.4.58
99	Unhand me, gentlemen	Ham 1.4.61
99	He waxes desperate with imagination	Ham 1.4.64
100	There may be in the cup	WT 2.1.41
101	Yield up, O love! Thy crown and hearted throne	Oth 3.3.452
101	... let her sport herself	WT 2.1.62
101	... strangle her in bed	Oth 4.1.202
101	Good, good; the justice of it pleases	Oth 4.1.204
101	Away with her to prison!	WT 2.1.105
102	Be certain what you do, sir	WT 2.1.129
103	I durst, my lord, to wager she is honest	Oth 4.2.13
103	... this most cruel usage of your queen	WT 2.3.117
104	Impudent strumpet!	Oth 4.2.84
104	My child? Away with it!	WT 2.3.132
104	If thou refuse And wilt encounter	WT 2.3.138
104	We enjoin thee	WT 2.3.173
105	It is the cause, it is the cause, my soul	Oth 5.2.1
105	she must die, else she'll betray more men	Oth 5.2.6
105	O perjur'd woman!	Oth 5.2.68
105	Let us be sacrificers, but not butchers	JC 2.1.166
105	It is the law, not I condemn your brother	MM 2.2.82
105	Is't not perfect conscience	Ham 5.2.68
106	Perdition catch my soul	Oth 3.3.91
106	Your actions are my dreams	WT 3.2.81
107	... so thou Shalt feel our justice	WT 3.2.88
107	The sessions shall proceed	WT 3.2.140
108	Prithee, bring me	WT 3.2.233
108	Try what repentance can: what can it not?	Ham 3.3.65
109	... the queen that bore thee	Mac 4.3.110
110	For do but stand upon the foaming shore	Oth 2.1.11
110	Blossom, speed thee well!	WT 3.3.45

110	... Farewell! The day frowns more and more	WT 3.3.52
110	Now bless thyself: thou mettest with things dying	WT 3.3.109
111	'Tis a lucky day, boy, and we'll do good deeds on't	WT 3.3.134
113	Even now I tremble	WT 4.4.18
113	... my desires Run not before mine honour	WT 4.4.33
113	O, but sir, Your resolution cannot hold	WT 4.4.35
114	Or I'll be thine, my fair	WT 4.4.42
114	For I cannot be	WT 4.4.43
115	To this I am most constant	WT 4.4.45
115	Mark your divorce, young sir	WT 4.4.417
116	If I may ever know thou dost but sigh	WT 4.4.427
116	I am but sorry, not afeared	WT 4.4.463
116	It cannot fail but by	WT 4.4.476
116	Camillo, Not for Bohemia	WT 4.4.487
117	Dear, look up	WT 5.1.214
118	Beseech you, sir	WT 5.1.217
118	So long could I	WT 5.3.84
119	... it is in my power	WT 4.1.7
120	Since Cassius first did whet me against Caesar	JC 2.1.61
120	Methought I heard a voice cry	Mac 2.2.33
120	Not poppy, nor mandragora	Oth 3.3.334
123	O Proserpina	WT 4.4.116
127	Pardon's the word to all	Cym 5.6.423
128	My honour'd lord, you know right well you did	Ham 3.1.99
129	... Or I'll be thine, my fair	WT 4.4.42
129	It cannot fail but by	WT 4.4.476
131	He, who the sword of heaven will bear	MM 3.1.517
133	How should I your true love know	Ham 4.5.23
133	Which bewept to the grave did not go	Ham 4.5.38
133	I hope all will be well	Ham 4.5.67
138	O! cursed, cursed slave	Oth 5.2.283
140	This above all: to thine own self be true	Ham 1.3.78
145	It is the law, not I, condemn your brother	MM 2.2.82
147	Mount, mount, my soul!	R2 5.5.111
148	I have been studying how I may compare	R2 5.5.1
150	At the last, Do as the heavens have done	WT 5.1.4
150	O! think on that	MM 2.2.79
161	You mar our labour ... You assist the storm	Tem 1.1.12
161	I pray thee, mark me	Tem 1.2.88
162	I have done nothing but in care of thee	Tem 1.2.16

Author's Other References

Page

3 'Shakespearean Tragedy', Lecture I, A.C. Bradley (Nineteenth century critic).

5 *William Shakespeare's Five-Act Structure*, T.W. Baldwin, University of Illinois Press, 1947.

64 *Crime and Punishment*, Dostoevsky.

81 'Two Essays on Analytical Psychology', *Collected Works*, Vol. VII, C.G. Jung

84 *The Wheel of Fire*, G. Wilson Knight, Oxford University Press, 1930.

119 *Shakespeare's Last Plays*, E.M.W. Tillyard, Chatto & Windus.

136 *The Allegory of Love*, C.S. Lewis.

140 *The Sacred Books of the East*, Vol. XIX, edited by Max Muller, Oxford, 1883.

157 'Psychology and Alchemy', *Collected Works*, Vol. XII, C.G. Jung.

141 *The Passion Play at Ober-Ammergau*, trans. Maria Trench, Kegan Paul, 1910.

149 *The Secret of the Golden Flower*, trans. R. Wilhelm, with a commentary by C.G. Jung.

151 *The Romaunt of the Rose*, Chaucer Society Texts, First Series, LXXXII.

154 *An Introduction to Jung's Psychology*, Frieda Fordham.

156 *The Divine Comedy*, Dante, *Purgatorio*, XXXI.

177 *The Bhagavad-Gita*, trans. Prabhavananda and Isherwood, intro. by Aldous Huxley.

192 'Anecdote for Fathers', Wordsworth.

Index